S0-DOP-251

Vincent Borremans has been writing about and playing golf (HCP 6) for twenty years. He is an international golf referee and tournament director, and golf correspondent for numerous magazines, newspapers, and broadcast media, including the European channel, Canal +.

First published in France by Editions Assouline, 1998

First published in the United States in 1998 by
UNIVERSE PUBLISHING
A Division of Rizzoli International Publications, Inc.
300 Park Avenue South, New York, NY 10010

ISBN: 0-7893-0139-3

Translated from the French by Chanterelle Translations, London
Typesetting: Chanterelle Translations
Photoengravng by Seleoffset, Italy
Printed and bound in Italy

GOLF

THE GAME AND ITS CHAMPIONS

VINCENT BORREMANS

UNIVERSE

CONTENTS

INTRODUCTION

Golf is going to be *the* game of the 21st century. Never before have there been so many players, spectators, and television viewers involved in the game. Of course, there are several reasons for this sudden enthusiasm, but much is due to the fact that golf is extremely telegenic. You don't have to be a great player to understand and feel the excitement of a tournament.

Golfing champions actually resemble their sport. In order to win at golf, you need to maintain an aggressive attitude. All the leading golfers thrive on the thrill of the hunt; in fact, many of the greatest players have been compared to predators of the wild—the hawk for Ben Hogan, the bear for Jack Nicklaus, the eagle for Severiano Ballesteros, and the great white shark for Greg Norman. Yet, the world of top golfing is a school of life, and despite players' latent aggression, the game's philosophy requires that players behave outwardly like gentlemen.

ANALYSIS OF MOVEMENT

Photo by Harold Edgerton.

The golf ball is too small for any player to control completely, and even champions can crack under pressure from one day to the next. Compared to other sports' heroes, golfers seem to remain in the prime of life forever; later in their careers they merely win fewer big matches. Jack Nicklaus won his first Grand Slam (the U.S. Open) when he was only 21 and, though he may still make a comeback, was still reeling off victories 25 years later. The Golden Bear, then 46 years of age, wore the green jacket for the sixth time eleven years after winning his first Masters.

Perhaps that is the secret of golf's popularity, the fact that it is "the sport of a lifetime." Once the casual beginner is introduced to the tiny round ball, he finds himself gripped by the game. Many of the values inherent in golf also explain its success. Playing any game is good for your health, and the challenge of exceeding one's personal best is an obvious incentive. Golf has the same rules and objectives for players at age seven or 77. The setting is a lush green, a magnificent spread of at least 250 acres without a building, a car, or pollution of any kind, and often inhabited by birds and game. Many golfers come and play during the week when fairways are blissfully quiet. It allows them to feel the course is their own, that for 18 holes they are alone in the world. A golfer, and even more so a champion golfer, is always an individualist.

The first evidence that people played a game hitting a ball into a hole dates from nearly 1,000 years ago. Though the great players of today's sport did not invent the game, their contribution is immeasurable. The public and the media are proof that the sport's astounding success is due largely to its champions. These great players—Ballesteros, for example, and Palmer before him—have aroused our emotions, surprised us, and made us rejoice. They have won loyal fans and rewarded them with heart-stopping moments of excitement. The popularity of the game is due as much to the champions' astounding expertise as it is to our desire to understand the players as individuals. Who are these athletes, and how did they reach their state of greatness?

THE FIRST THIRTEEN RULES

Written down by John Rattray of the Honorable Company of Edinburgh Golfers in 1744.

6

Articles & Laws in playing the Golf

1 You must Tee your Ball within a Club length of the Hole

2 Your Tee must be upon the Ground

3 You are not to change the Ball which you Strike off the Tee

4 You are not to remove Stones, Bones or any Break Club for the
   Sake of playing your Ball Except upon the fair Green,
   and that only within a Club length of your Ball.

5 If your Ball comes among Water, or any Watery filth, You are at
   Liberty to take out your Ball, and ~~throw~~ ^bringing^ it behind the
   Hazard ~~and teeing it~~ ^6 yards at least^, You may play it with any Club, and
   allow your Adversary a Stroke, for so getting out your Ball.

6 If your Balls be found any where touching ~~one~~ another, You are to lift
   the first Ball, till You play the last.

7 At Holeing, You are to play Your Ball honestly for the Hole, and
   not to play upon your Adversaries Ball, not lying in your way to the Hole

8 If you should lose your Ball, by its being taken up, or any other way
   You are to go back to the Spot, where you Struck last, and drop
   another Ball, and Allow your Adversary a Stroke for the Misfortune

9 No Man at Holeing his Ball, is to be Allowed to Mark his way
   to the Hole with his Club or any thing else.

10 If a Ball be Stop'd by any person, Horse, Dog, or any thing else, the
    Ball so Stop'd must be played where it lyes.

11 If you Draw your Club in Order to Strike, and proceed so far in the Stroke
    as to be bringing down your Club; if then your Club shall
    break, in any way, it is to be Accounted a Stroke.

12 He, whose Ball lyes furthest from the Hole is Obliged to play first

13 Neither Trench, Ditch, or Dyke made for the preservation of the
    Links, Nor the Scholars Holes or the Soldiers Lines shall be
    Accounted a Hazard, But the Ball is to be taken out, Teed
    and played with any Iron Club.

HISTORY

The game of "choule" and "colf"

The relationship between man and ball is as old as the Earth itself. Most probably, the game of "choule," or "chole" (pronounced "shool") is the basis for the modern game of golf. Choule was played in the 13th century in northern France and in Flanders over the flat countryside by two teams using a single ball. The Dutch historian, S. Van Hengel, places the first round of "colf" in Loenen in 1297. Two teams of four players competed to hit their ball at a target consisting of a marker point over a distance of about three miles. For years, many cities forbade the playing of colf due to the damage caused by the balls, and eventually the game was only allowed to be played on the ice during severe winters.

Colf disappeared at the beginning of the 18th century, when it was replaced by "kolf." This game was played over much shorter distances, and can thus take credit for being

JOHN McDERMOTT IN 1911

First American winner of the U.S. Open.

ALLAN ROBERTSON

The first "great golfer," a contemporary of Old Tom Morris.

WHY EIGHTEEN HOLES?

The links used by the St. Andrews club made it possible to play 11 holes along St. Andrew's Bay right up to the River Eden. By using double green, one could double the distance by playing a "round" (there and back) of 22 holes. In about 1764, after the club's first few years in existence, it condensed the first four holes (there and back) into two, reducing the course to 18 holes. When the club became the Royal St. Andrews in 1834, it defeated the rival Honorable Company of Edinburgh Golfers for dominance of the game, although Edinburgh had been the first to publish rules and hold a competition. In 1858, St. Andrews fixed the 18-hole standard once and for all.

ST. ANDREWS

Robert Fargan's workshop in 1890.

the earliest form of golf. It is likely that in the 14th century, the game of choule was introduced into England and Scotland. Soldiers from these countries would have learned the game through military expeditions into France. But it was mainly in Scotland that the game took shape. It soon evolved into "gowff" or "golfe," practiced on the links on the east coast of Scotland, though the rules of the game were not codified until as late as the early 18th century.

Freemasonry and the Concept of the Club

As in the case of colf, the records of golf's early years are sparse, but the game was clearly popular. Anyone could play on the links; all one needed was a club and a ball. The foundations of the modern game were established by the freemasons who introduced golf into their secret meetings, often ending in a lavish feast. There's nothing like a brisk walk taken while playing a game to whet the appetite. Since bets were often

taken, everyone needed to play by the same rules. The freemasons established a code whereby members shared everything as fairly as possible (hence the "fair" as in "fairway"). The first club, the Edinburgh Burgess Golfing Society, was founded in 1735. Very few records survive because the freemasons' lodge destroyed all the archives to prevent its rites and secrets from being revealed. All that we know is that membership was drawn from wide social circles, as one finds names of lawyers and bankers next to those of glaziers and bakers.

In 1744, the Honorable Company of Edinburgh Golfers was founded. This body offered a prize for a competition over the Leith links, a five-hole course just outside the city. Thirteen rules were laid down. The Edinburgh golfing society moved to the Musselburgh links in 1836 and finally settled at the Muirfield course in 1891.

The equipment and balls soon became more sophisticated. Since club members tended to be aristocrats or from the wealthy middle classes, they had the means to pay for "featheries," expensive, handmade balls crafted from a tophatful of boiled goose feathers packed inside a sheepskin casing.

The St. Andrews Golfing Society

Clubs of golfing freemasons soon multiplied. Another golfing society was formed at St. Andrews in 1754, and these members played on the common lands made available by the city for all its inhabitants. Freemasons' clubs began to play on privately owned land so they wouldn't be disturbed by non-members. Golf became a second office for businessmen and merchants, and the club was used to hold unofficial business meetings.

Golf Crosses the Scottish Borders

When traders and sailors leave their native shores to trade in foreign lands, they take their favorite pastimes with them. Golf's first "foreign" bridgehead was established in 1818 in Manchester, England, a major financial center. A few years later, the famous Old Tom Morris was brought in to redesign the 18 holes of the Kersal Moor course. This was actually the second English course after the Royal Blackheath, created by expatriate Scotsmen just south of London. Yet 100 years after the first golfing societies were formed in Scotland, there were only two other clubs beyond its borders. The third still exists in its original 1864 form. The Royal North Devon, also called the Westward Ho! Club, greatly benefited from the publication of the results of Scotland's first Open Championships in 1860.

The fact that the game of golf was played in the open air became one of its best features.

ALLAN ROBERTSON (CARRYING HIS CLUBS, ON THE LEFT)

(Preceding pages) *Prestwick organized the first Open in 1860 in his memory.*

HARRY VARDON IN 1895

Six-times winner of the British Open and a grip which bears his name have made him a legend.

15

It received another impetus when a new type of ball was invented, which was made of gutta percha, the rubbery resin of a tropical tree. This made the sport easier to play and, more importantly, much less expensive. New facilities were also introduced. Clubs were no longer content merely to own a course, they needed a clubhouse where they could meet, change clothes, and eat and drink in comfort.

The First Champions

Allan Robertson and Old Tom Morris were the earliest champions. As soon as there were enough clubs and competitors to organize a competition worthy of the name, championships were held. In 1858, Robertson shot a 79 at the Old Course, making him the first to play the course in less than 80. Old Tom Morris won his fourth and last Open in 1867 at the age of 46, which still remains a record. In 1860, Prestwick began holding an Open, the winner of which was awarded a red belt. The "Belt" was awarded to the first man to win the Open three times running. The first recipient was none other than Young Tom Morris, son of Old Tom, who won a series of Opens (1868, '69, '70) on the Prestwick course and was the first player to achieve a hole-in-one in the history of the Open (later known as the British Open). The "Claret Jug," a silver wine jug, later replaced the Belt as the trophy.

Harry Vardon, the Six-Open Invincible

At the turn of the century, Harry Vardon popularized a new way of holding the club, using an overlapping grip in which the little finger of the right hand was placed on top of the left hand (for right-handed golfers). Vardon played in tournaments in the United States to promote new types of golf balls. Crowds flocked to see his virtuosity and his new style of grip.

The future major manufacturer of clubs at St. Andrews, Willie Auchterlonie, won the Open in 1893. The first foreigner to win the coveted Claret Jug was, in fact, a Frenchman, Arnaud Massy, who won it at Hoylake in 1907. It was not until the Ballesteros's victory in 1979 that a Continental player won the famous trophy again.

In 1920, the six clubs that hosted the most important Tour of the period decided to entrust the organization of the Open to one Club, St. Andrews. One year later, Jock Hutchinson, who was actually Scottish-born, was the first American to win "The Open." In the United States in 1913, an unknown American amateur, Francis Ouimet, won the U.S. Open, beating the Scottish professional to break the British

TOM VARDON

(Previous pages) *Coming second in the British Open, standing behind his brother Harry, watched by James Braid.*

MARRIAGE OF THE R&A AND THE USGA

St. Andrews became a royal club, in 1834 and each time a new club opened, it adopted the rules of the R&A rather than those of the Gentlemen Golfers of Leith of 1744. The revised rules were published in 1891 with the addition of new articles. The Royal and Ancient thus became established as the sole arbiter worldwide, with the exception of the U.S. and Mexico.

When in 1894, five clubs banded together to create the United States Golfing Association (USGA), Charles Blair Macdonald, son of a Scottish immigrant, insisted that the two associations join forces in setting the rules of the game. This union was more of a marriage of convenience than of mutual regard. The traditionalist R&A balked at making minor modifications and feared losing its influence over the game. In 1950, the two associations nearly broke apart, and the battle began over which would have the final say in creating the official rules. In 1984, the two bodies finally combined their interpretations into *Decisions on the Rules of Golf*, now amended every four years.

WILLIE AUCHTERLONIE

Carrying the seven clubs which won him the 1893 Open.

BOB JONES IN 1930

The year of the Grand Slam.

reign on American soil. The path was now open for Walter Hagen. Ouimet was the forerunner of numerous other amateur winners of the U.S. Open, such as Travis (1915), Evans (1916), Jones (1923, '26, '29, '30), and Goodman (1933). American amateurs have since remained almost unbeatable by their British and Irish opponents in Walker Cup meets. Only recently Scott Verplank, the U.S. Amateur Champion in 1984, won a professional match on the U.S. circuit, the Western Open, in 1986. The careers of Phil Mickelson, Justin Leonard, and Tiger Woods are further examples of the importance of amateur golf in the United States. The opportunity offered by colleges and universities is one of the major reasons for their success.

The Decisive Role of the Development of the Golf Ball

The more reliable and less costly the ball, the more popular golf became. Up until 1848, the "featheries" made of a leather sheath filled with boiled feathers were far too fragile, and cost almost as much as a club. They were subsequently replaced by a ball made of a natural resin called gutta percha. This meant the balls could be mass-produced by being poured into individual molds. However, even gutta percha had some

BOB JONES

While remaining an amateur, he revolutionized the game of golf worldwide.

disadvantages as it could burst when hit hard. Then, an American named Colin Haskell invented a revolutionary type of ball which consisted of a rubber core surrounded by an elastic band, inside a gutta-percha shell. He had it made at the Goodrich factory. The Haskell ball soon overtook the "Gutty" in popularity in the early 20th century. It went farther, had a better feel, and was cheaper to produce. The rubber core was soon replaced by a hollow center filled with liquid; balata, a natural rigid resin, was used for the outer casing. The Dunlop 31, introduced in 1912, was the first ball of this type on the market, which it soon dominated.

In 1921, the R&A defined the characteristics of the ball. The size was to be 1.62 inches in diameter, and it was not to weigh more than 1.62 ounces. Urged on by new golfers, the USGA was won over by a larger ball (1.68 inches in diameter), which makes it easier for the average golfer to play. The United States opted for a different standard, taking into account the masses who ultimately determine the popularity of the sport. This attitude has undoubtedly been key to the sport's success in the United States.

The U.S. also accepted the use of steel shafts for clubs nearly five years before this took place in Scotland (1924–1929). But the story behind the size of the ball is even more

extraordinary. The USGA introduced the larger ball in 1932, but its use was only authorized alongside the smaller one in 1951 and it took until January 1, 1990, for this rule to be adopted by courses throughout the world. The small ball is well-suited to links by the seashore. It doesn't fly as high, rolls further, and can be hooked or sliced more effectively. These three attributes are an advantage for good players, but place other players at a disadvantage. In addition, the small ball does not work as well on inland courses. Although golf is mostly played a long way from the sea in the United Kingdom, the R&A was never willing to admit this prior to the 1950 decision, and never accepted the preference of continental Europe for the larger ball.

The Globalization of Golf

At the turn of the century, some 500 clubs were created in Great Britain, both in big cities and at the seaside. Yet unlike colf and kolf, golf was a sport reserved for those who could pay the high membership fees demanded by private clubs. Clubs had come

a long way from their democratic beginnings, and investment in them had become substantial. Clubhouses were built and man-made courses were created.

Continental Europe discovered golf through their cross-Channel neighbors in 1856 at Pau, in southwestern France, where the British laid out a course. Thirty years later, in 1888, the British opened Belgium's first golf club in Antwerp. The Hague, Bad Homburg, and Baden Baden soon followed.

Meanwhile, golf began to be played in Australia (1869), New Zealand (1871), Canada (1875), the United States (1888), Ceylon (1890), Malaya (1893), and Hong Kong by the end of the century. In 1901, Golf first reached the Land of the Rising Sun when a course was opened near Kobe, the foot of Mount Rokko. Between the opening of the Adelaide Golf Club in 1870 and the end of the century, Australia opened 12 clubs, while its little neighbor, New Zealand, boasted 18. Canada stole a march of several years on the United States; the Ontario and Montreal clubs started up as long ago as 1875.

HENRY COTTON AT THE SANDWICH COURSE, 1934

The last great British player before Nick Faldo swept all before him 50 years later.

HISTORY

The Amazing Story of Golf in the United States

Freemasons who emigrated from Scotland in the 18th century continued their golfing activities in the Deep South, in Carolina, Georgia, and Maryland, but it was not until a Scot took the initiative in 1888 that the first miniature course (consisting first of three holes, later of six) was created in Yonkers, just outside New York.

The club founded by John Reid was nicknamed "The Old Apple Tree Gang" with the most famous apple tree in the golfing world serving as the clubhouse. The official name of the club was the St. Andrew's Golf Club (note the slightly different spelling from that of the city of St. Andrews, Scotland), but it wasn't until 1897 that it acquired the full 18 holes. Although legend tends to honor Reid for founding the first golf course, several other courses in the northern states claim precedence. Shinnecock Hills (1891) was the first to have a real clubhouse. Designed by the master craftsman and Scottish golfing professional, Willie Dunn, this Long Island club had two separate miniature courses, 12 holes for men and nine for women. The two courses were occasionally combined, as in 1896 when the club hosted the second U.S. Open. Dunn met some American golfers in Biarritz in 1890 where he was designing the second French golf course and they persuaded him to become the first Scottish pro to emigrate to the United States.

The inventions of Edison and Ford boosted economic activity considerably in the United States, and the movers and shakers of the time found they needed a leisure activity to bring them together. Golf became that vehicle. After the initial trail had been blazed, hundreds of new clubs sprang up like mushrooms.

A journalist named Tom Bendelow, profiting from this niche market, designed nearly 600 courses. Bendelow, a Scotsman, was behind the opening of several of the public courses in the United States. Some were built with a budget of only $25 a hole. The importance of his work can be judged today, in that certain European countries, such as Italy and Belgium, still have no public courses. Champions such as Florey Van Donck, Donald Swaelens, and Umberto Grappasonni are unknown in their own country, and it was not until the 1980s that France had its first public courses.

A Thousand New Clubs in the Last Decade of 19th Century

As the clubs proliferated, so did golfing competitions. The Scots dominated the early years of golfing in the United States and it wasn't until Johnny McDermott's victory in 1911 that the U.S. Open was finally won by an American-born player.

SAM SNEAD

Captain and player, seen here in 1953.

RACIAL DISCRIMINATION: THE SHAME OF THE U.S. TOUR

The U.S. Tour was openly racist for 66 years, from 1865 through 1961, by refusing to allow any non-Caucasian to join the Association. The first golfing martyr was John Shippen, who was half-Black, half-Native American. At the second U.S. Open, played at Shinnecock Hills in 1895, white American and British immigrant participants opposed his registration and threatened to boycott the event. The first defender of human rights was President of the USGA, Theodore Havemeyer, who bravely allowed Shippen to take part. Nevertheless, non-whites were long barred from private clubs and the ranks of the professionals. The world-famous boxers, Sugar Ray Robinson and Joe Louis, both of whom were enthusiastic golfers, also suffered discrimination. For the best black players of the time, such as Ted Rhodes and Bill Spiller, the only way to get to play was to receive an invitation. George May was one of the first to be able to do so in the Tam O'Shanter World Invitational. In practice, nothing extraordinary occurred until Stanley Mosk, Attorney General of the State of California, took action, prohibiting golf tournaments to be held within his state. This was enough to make the PGA think again and in 1961 the racial laws of the Tour were finally abolished. In 1969, Charlie Sifford was the first non-white to win an event in the Tour, the Los Angeles Open, but he was never invited to play in the Masters. Clifford Robberts waited ten years to see Lee Elder play at Augusta in 1974. It wasn't until as recently as 1990 that the PGA refused to hold tournament events in "Whites Only" clubs.

A CROWD AROUND THE 18TH AT ST. ANDREWS

(Following pages) *The British Open, July 1927.*

GENE SARAZEN IN 1935

Above right, "The Squirrel," twenty years after he played the famous albatross at Augusta.

JOHN FITZGERALD KENNEDY'S GOLF BAG

The American president used Ben Hogan's Power Thrust clubs.

The second Industrial Revolution in the early 1920s provided the decisive impetus for the future domination of the game by the United States. British domination had ended forever, except for the role it has continued to play in the codifying and interpretation of the rules, through the Royal and Ancient Golf Club of St. Andrews.

The Concept of Captain

The first captaincy dates from 1744, when the first competition was held. The winner of the Silver Club trophy automatically became known as Captain for a year. It was his job to settle disputes between players during his term. When the prize was awarded, the Captain had to pledge a financial guarantee of 50 pounds, a sizable sum at the time. He would only get his money back when he returned the Silver Club, just before next year's competition!

Golfing Architecture Still Dominated by the Scots

The Scots deserve credit for their extraordinary influence on course design for the first 40 years of this century. Inspired by the great layouts and scenery of their native land (such as Dornoch, St. Andrews, and Prestwick), they set out to create the most beautiful courses in the world. They were fortunate to be able to choose from sites which were as challenging for the players as they were breathtakingly beautiful. Donald Ross and Alister Mackenzie are the spiritual heirs of the first golf course architects, Willie Park, Jr. and Old Tom Morris. Ross was responsible for, among others, Pinehurst #2, Oakland Hills, Seminole, Inverness, and Worcester, all in the United States. Mackenzie can count courses such as Augusta, Cypress Point, and the Royal Melbourne as his best work. For their part, the English found in Tom Simpson and Harry Colt the ideal designers to shape their finest courses. In the United States, George Crump (Pine Valley), Charles Blair Macdonald (National Golf Club), Jack Neville (Pebble Beach), Hugh Wilson (Merion), and Albert Tillinghast (Winged Foot, Baltusrol) created legendary courses, though none were golf course designers by training. Much later, in the 1960s, Robert Trent Jones, Pete Dye, George Fazio, and shortly thereafter his nephew, Tom Fazio, created a new type of course layout which was designed with professional competitions in mind. Trent Jones introduced the idea of creating courses from scratch. His new philosophy of course design would incorporate the now standard ingredients of water hazards, sand traps (or bunkers), banks, and hollows.

BEN HOGAN

(Facing) *A life in the service of his swing.*

J.F.K. AND BENJAMIN BRADLEY AT THE DRIVE, NEWPORT, RHODE ISLAND

32   (Previous pages) *Seen here with their wives (September 13, 1963).*

The Great Golfers Win Media Attention

From the early 1920s, the great golfers began to hit the headlines. On his arrival in New York after winning the British Open in 1926, Bobby Jones was honored with a ticker-tape parade. As a professor emeritus of golf, he revolutionized the sport worldwide yet remained an amateur as he didn't need to earn his living in competition. In 1930, at the age of 28, he retired at the height of his fame, having won four victories in the Grand Slam. No one has ever equaled that incredible record. Bobby Jones was adored by the Scots as much for his delightful personality as for his supreme mastery of the sport. The Americans used to say of Bob Jones that he brought everything back to his country: his unequaled glory, the Augusta course, and the Masters.

Among the professionals of his era, Walter Hagen stands out as combining performance and elegance. Hagen was a natty dresser and flamboyant personality who loved attention, unlike his more retiring opponent, Gene Sarazen, the son of an Italian immigrant. In Europe, only Henry Cotton was able to put up a creditable resistance to Hagen. Cotton and Hagen were the first men to change the image of the golf professional. The United Kingdom had to wait for the likes of Tony Jacklin and Nick Faldo to once again breed champions of the caliber of Sir Henry Cotton. Sarazen, whose real name was Eugenio Saraceni, put the Augusta Masters on the map thanks to the albatross (hole in five) he played at the 15th hole in the last round, enabling him to force a playoff and ultimately win. His second contribution to the game was the invention of the sand wedge. He had the idea that if he made the head of the niblick heavier, he could hit the ball out of a sand trap more easily.

The 1940s and Byron Nelson

The 1940s saw the emergence of several great champions. No one could get in the way of Byron Nelson's driving ambition. Between 1940 through 1947, he broke an impressive number of records, many never equaled. He played 113 rounds without missing a cut and shot under 70 on 19 courses in a row. In his 11 victories in a row in 1945, his average score was 68.33. "Lord Byron" was a hemophiliac and thus exempt from military service, which explains his brilliant career in the United States and the fact that he never encountered any European opposition. Even after 1946, despite the advent of Ben Hogan and Sam Snead,

ARNOLD PALMER

(Following pages) *Images of a great champion.*

no one could beat this golfing giant. Nelson played ceaselessly, and perhaps overdid it. His career ended in 1947. Today, his impressive swing is remembered and recreated by the ball-testing machine which bears his name—The Iron Nelson.

Ben "The Hawk" Hogan's Tragic Destiny

Ben Hogan was raised modestly by his mother who had been widowed when her husband committed suicide in front of nine-year-old Ben. He spent his youth earning tips caddying on the course in Fort Worth, Texas, like his friend Byron Nelson. The young Texan was gauche, though gifted. He started playing tournaments when he was in his twenties, earning just enough to pay for his trips. Having analyzed the

THE THREE MUSKETEERS OF MODERN GOLF: PALMER, NICKLAUS, AND PLAYER

This triumvirate is the true foundation of modern golf. While the Scottish freemasons played a dominant role in the birth of the game and the R&A and the USGA enabled golf to grow, these three champions laid the foundations of the sport today. Palmer created the legend of the golfing champion, making an enormous impact on golf's public image through marketing and the media. Nicklaus imposed professionalism both on and off the course. Finally, Player introduced the virtues of mental and physical strength, determination, and preparation.

ARNOLD PALMER

Leading his huge fanclub.

35

NICKLAUS, PALMER, AND NORMAN

The three titans of golfing history.

TOM WATSON AND JACK NICKLAUS

Between them they have been responsible for some of golf's finest moments.

GARY PLAYER ON THE SENIOR TOUR

His determination remains intact.

golf swing in all its manifestations, Ben invented the "power fade" and the practice shot. At age 34, "The Hawk" won admiration for all of his hard work and perseverance. In February 1949, at the height of his fame, Ben Hogan was the victim of a near-fatal car accident and stopped playing for 15 months. Although his legs were never the same again, in 1950, he won the U.S. Open at Merion, and in 1953 won the U.S. Open at Oakmont, followed by the British Open at Carnoustie. Yet the man who never left anything to chance would never check out distances, maps of the course, or flag positions. He did everything by feel. "The general assessment made by your eyes ought to be enough," he would say, "I'm against all that extra information."

The Age of Arnold Palmer or the Media Revolution

The postwar boom reawakened an interest in golf that was already being reinforced by other factors. Television had discovered the sport and its magnificent courses. It also discovered personalities, such as the great Arnold Palmer. Palmer soon became a national hero accompanied by a horde of fans known as "Arnie's Army." When Hollywood stars, such as Bing Crosby and Bob Hope, began to create their own tournaments, the sport found itself in the spotlight of attention nationwide. Sports promoter Mark McCormack helped Palmer to profit from the interest in the champion shown by golfers, and television

LEE TREVINO

His sense of humor and imagination has gotten him out of lots of tight corners.

viewers, and the corporations wanted to link their image with his. It was U.S. President Dwight D. Eisenhower, who, in the late 1950s, proudly displayed his passion for golf, part-nering Palmer in charity matches.

The European Divide

While the United States was creating champion after champion, top-level golf in Europe was at a crisis point throughout the 1950s and 1960s. Golf in Europe was still a game played only by the elite. Florey Van Donck (Belgium), Ramon Sota (Spain), and Umberto Grappasonni (Italy) remained anonymous despite their strings of victories. Max Faulkner, Peter Alliss, Bernard Hunt, Brian Hugget, Neil Coles, Christy O'Connor, and Dai Rees were the British and Irish standard-bearers of the period.

The Golden Sixties and the Golden Bear

In the early 1960s, an amateur from Colombus, Ohio, emerged onto the scene. His name was Jack Nicklaus. Very soon, he was matched against Arnold Palmer. "How dare this young upstart attempt to attack our idol?" cried the Palmer army of sup-porters. Nicklaus was a workaholic, inspired by Ben Hogan. Between them, Nicklaus and Palmer smashed any opposition; only Gary Player managed to keep up with the two American champions. Nicklaus won more matches than anyone, and in 1988 was awarded the title, "Best Golfer of the Century." He never used to be a very long hitter of the ball , but unlike Hogan or Snead, he was an excellent putter and could extricate himself from bunkers like no one else. It's hardly surprising to learn that he has inspired Severiano Ballesteros.

Watson, Trevino, De Vincenzo, and the Crazy Seventies

Player and Nicklaus would stay on top for three decades! Only the Argentinian Roberto De Vicenzo, the Englishman Tony Jacklin, and the Japanese Isao Aoki gave the American giant some cause for concern. A few newcomers to the U.S. Tour did occasionally grab a piece of the action. Raymond Floyd counted on the precision of his iron drives and putting and Johnny Miller had a terrific time in the 1970s when he won two Majors (the U.S. Open in 1973 and the British Open in 1976), but his career only lasted ten years, a short one compared with that of other champions.

Miller and Lee Trevino are direct opposites. Lee Trevino has fed on golfing myths since the 1960s. Trevino's amazing swing has helped make the American dream come true for him. He devised his own special swing on the public courses of Texas, while his depth of concentration enables him to immerse himself completely in the shot three seconds before he plays it. Between shots, he spends his time chatting and telling the best jokes on the Tour. Trevino is a one-of-a-kind, a true individual, and the subject of one of the greatest chapters of golfing history.

Watson and Nicklaus Battle it Out

Nicklaus's great rival was born in Kansas. Tom Watson won eight Majors, including an unforgettable final victory in the British Open at Turnberry in 1977. Watson was very much at ease on the Scottish courses and has won five times between 1975 and 1983. In the late 1980s, luck turned against him in the short game. Like Sam Snead, Ben Hogan, and Tony Jacklin, Watson could never sink a putt. He had to wait until the mid-1990s to win on the U.S. Tour (the 1996 Memorial Tournament). Floyd won the U.S. Open at the age of 43, Nicklaus won the Masters in 1986 at the age of 46, Watson won on the Tour 20 years after his first victory, and Trevino won the U.S. PGA after a gap of ten years. These champions have staying power because they apply the strict rules of professionalism. Improvisation is out of the question on today's Tour.

THE CHAMPIONS

The best pros on the Tour have been working to make the modern game a success for the past two hundred years. They include Palmer, Nicklaus, and Ballesteros, the main movers and shakers thanks to the pioneering work done by Walter Hagen and Harry Vardon in the 1930s.

All of the champions whose careers are discussed in these pages are capable of transforming a competition into a flamboyant firework display, awarding spectators unforgettable moments of excitement. Although these stars share the desire to win, they are by no means alike in other ways. The key to golf's success is this alchemy which brings outstanding players together who have such different temperaments and personalities, all in the service of the sport. It is this variety which attracts the public and they in turn attract advertisers and sponsors, who keep the whole show on the road.

ROBERT TYRE JONES

The only champion to have won the Grand Slam (1930).

severiano

BALLESTEROS

HIS FIRST BRITISH OPEN, AGED 18, AT THE ROYAL BIRKDALE

1976 British Open. It ended with a shot from Johnny Miller.

When histories of golf are written, Seve Ballesteros will be portrayed as the man who single-handedly revived the fortunes of European golf. Ballesteros emerged on the international scene in the mid-1970s. "Seve," whose name is pronounced "Sebe," in his native Spanish, inspired a whole generation of European champions who were born in the same year, 1957. Faldo, Langer, Woosnam, Lyle, and the Australian Greg Norman all emerged as world-class golfers. Ballesteros is not only the best player of the 1980s; his captaincy of the Ryder Cup, played at Valderrama in 1997, is indicative of his key role in the European golfing scene.

An Unusual Personality

A native of Pedrena, on Spain's Atlantic coast, Ballesteros has never been motivated by such altruistic concerns as a desire to become the "spiritual father of Europe," as he is sometimes known. He has always pursued his personal goals, and decided from an early age that he would always play things his way. Unlike Tiger Woods, Ballesteros is a lone wolf. In the early 1970s, Spain was considered by the British golfing elite to

(Previous) *Ballesteros as Ryder Cup team captain.*

HIS FIRST MAJOR

Royal Lytham & St. Anne's, July, 1979.

be a nation of minimal importance somewhere way down south on the European mainland. Seve would never forget the discrimination he experienced and was determined that he would never be prevented from becoming the world's number one.

Passion, Imagination, Individualism, and Pride

These typically Spanish personality traits are found in bullfighters. Severiano understood from a very young age that his bull-ring would be the golf course, his banderilla the putter. From the age of seven, Seve, the son of rowing champion Baldomero Ballesteros, would imitate the golf swings of his brothers and his uncle, the professional Ramon Sota, on the beach. By playing on such a difficult surface with a rusty old three-iron head mounted on a stick, Seve developed an exceptional touch and learned to create shots that would get him out of difficult

THE MASTERS AT AUGUSTA

(Following pages) *He has the magic touch which is ideal for this type of course.*

THE 1979 CLARET JUG

Start of the Age of Ballesteros.

SEVERIANO BALLESTEROS

BORN APRIL 9, 1957
AT PEDRENA, SPAIN

MARRIED, 3 CHILDREN

5 MAJORS
BRITISH OPEN 1979-84-88
MASTERS 1980-83

72 PRO WINS

RYDER CUP
1979-83-85-87-89-91-93-95

CAPTAIN IN 1997

LIVES AT PEDRENA, SPAIN

positions. He became a great admirer of Gary Player, and like him, spent hours practicing, often very early in the morning. He stayed in shape by doing a lot of cycling.
Like the South African, Seve adopted the habit of wearing a dark color (dark blue, in
his case) on the last day of a tournament.

Talent and Will Power Overcome Adversity

When, in 1974, Seve was given a set of clubs by an American soldier and $1,000 from
Dr. Cesar Campuzano, a member of the Santander Golf Club, he left his amateur sta-
tus behind. His life as a professional had begun, and he set off on his quest for victory
and international recognition. His first pro competition outside Spain was the 1974
Open in Portugal. Win or lose, Seve went home between competitions and drew
strength from his family, especially his three brothers, Baldomero, Manuel, and
Vicente, all of them golfing professionals (his fourth brother died very young from a
wasp sting). The first disappointments were humiliating, but Ballesteros picked himself up and came in fifth in the Italian Open. The young player eventually came to the
notice of Argentinian Roberto De Vincenzo, who found him an American manager,
Ed Barner. The kid from Pedrena was about to get the chance to compete against the
best players in the world on the U.S. circuit.

The Spanish Palmer, the Tiger Woods of the 1970s

Ballesteros did not do particularly well however, and returned to Europe, where his
luck soon changed. His first victory was in Holland in 1976, followed by wins in Belgium, France, England, Switzerland, Germany, and Scandinavia. Seve won his first
Major, the British Open, at the Royal Lytham and St. Anne's in 1979.
In Ballesteros a legend has been born: his drives are long, and he has a talent for extricating himself from impossible situations; his swing is balanced by a classic stance; he
produces shots that no one else does, and is a great putter under pressure. Seve is an artist
(he even played fifteen tournaments in a row without three-putting), and an exceptionally
brave man.

BRITISH OPEN 1989, ST. ANDREWS

(Facing page) *A determination to win: victory is all that counts.*

THE MAGICIAN OF THE TOUR

(Following pages) *Creative and gifted, he manages to extricate himself from the most dangerous situations.*

53

" Europe owes a debt to Severiano which it will probably never be able to repay."

ROYAL LYTHAM & ST. ANNE'S, 1988

One of his brilliant strokes which denied victory to Nick Price.

WITH JOSÉ-MARIA OLAZÁBAL IN THE 1989 RYDER CUP

United in joy and sadness.

A Feeling of Discrimination

Ballesteros's strong character has led him to take on many of the official institutions of the tour. American players receive a certain amount of money before each competition, the so-called "guarantee fee." When Seve asked for the same from Ken Schofield, who ran the European Tour, he was turned down. Seve was subsequently invited to play in two lucrative competitions in Japan, but Schofield forbade him to go. That was too much, and Ballesteros resigned from the PGA. The British pros took their revenge by leaving him off of the Ryder Cup team in 1981. Seve was enraged but did not want to become a permanent expatriate, spending his life in either London or the United States. Neither the U.S. Tour nor the European Tour would allow him to play in the other, as is now permitted. The autocratic Deane Beman would also not allow him to play in more than six tournaments on the circuit in 1985. The pressure he was under certainly contributed to his defeat in the Masters in 1985 and 1986.

BALLESTEROS AND OLAZÁBAL: THE DREAM DUO

Their secret: putting with eyes and heart.

AN INTIMIDATING LOOK

Dak Hill Country Club, Ryder Cup, 1995.

Ballesteros suffered a different kind of discrimination in Spain. In 1982, he fell in love with Carmen Bottin, daughter of a wealthy banker. Carmen's family was opposed to a liaison with a sportsman of humble origins. Severiano set out to prove he was worthy to be the son-in-law of a Spanish grandee. He became the number-one player in the world and his bank balance swelled accordingly. He married Carmen in 1988, and they have three children, Baldomero (1990), Miguel (1992), and Carmen (1994).

Five Majors and 72 Victories All Over the World

Ballesteros became the youngest-ever winner of the British Open in 1979, and rewrote the record books in 1980 when he won the Masters at only twenty-three years, three days. It was a classic victory in true Ballesteros style. His drives went all over the course, rarely landing on the fairways, but his extraordinary short game always brought him to the flag. This display enthralled the gallery, who watched him follow a succession of birdies with several bogeys. Ballesteros pulled off another feat three years later when he beat Ben Crenshaw and Tom Kite. These were the great "Seve" years when he was

WITH TONY JACKLIN: THE 1985 RYDER CUP VICTORY

Revenge of the two players who were left out of the selection for too long.

considered to be the best player in the world. He won the British Open in 1984 at St. Andrews and had many other victories, including the World Match Play. He won his last Major, the British Open, in 1988 at the Royal Lytham and St. Anne's, where he had made his debut as a winner in the Grand Slam. Playing against Nick Price, his final round of 65 has gone down in history, and he considers it his best performance. Ballesteros admits to having a few regrets in terms of missing trophies, including the U.S. Open, U.S. PGA, and the Masters in 1985, 1986, and 1987.

Without Him There Would Be No More Ryder Cup

Seve made his debut in 1979 with fellow Spaniard Antonio Garrido—the first two Continentals to break the British monopoly. Jack Nicklaus warned the British PGA that without the introduction of new talent such as Ballesteros to the European team, the event would lose all its glamour. His beginnings were modest. After the 1981 setback, Seve gained attention in 1983 in his match against Fuzzy Zoeller. He hit one of the best shots ever played, according to Nicklaus, using a three-wood to get out of

a sand trap. Seve drew in that match and realized that Europe was close to winning. The next chapter has gone down in history. For the first time in twenty-eight years, the U.S. bit the dust. The man behind the victory was Severiano Ballesteros. In 1987, he added a new dimension to the game, forming a partnership with fellow-Spaniard Olazábal that proved to be magic. Together, teacher and student brought down the American team. They cleaned up more than twelve points in the competition between 1987 and 1993. Then came 1995, a black year for Spanish golfing. Olazábal developed a mysterious injury that prevented him from walking, and Ballesteros completely lost his form.

Captain of Valderrama

As the captain of a European team in transition, one which was much weaker on paper than its rival, Seve needed to draw on all his cunning strategies and legendary courage. Spain became the first country outside

WITH BUTCH HARMON, KNOWN AS DOCTOR SWING

Tiger Woods and Seve shared the same coach.

THE SAME ATTITUDE PREVAILS ON THE GREENS
The same grip, the same position, and the same technique have stood Seve in good stead for 25 years.

A ROYAL FAN, VALDERRAMA, 1997

King Juan Carlos gave his personal backing to Seve throughout the Ryder Cup.

the British Isles to host the Ryder Cup. The honor of Spain as well as Seve's own reputation were at stake. If he failed, the British press would not spare him and the sneers from golfing officialdom would have been unbearable. Seve gave his all and his bet paid off. The European team won the Cup and the entire event was brilliantly organized. Ballesteros's recipe was simple: he had to be everywhere all the time and inspire everyone with his mental and physical powers. The energy of this forty-year-old man is truly amazing. The American press has claimed that, without Ballesteros, Europe would never have been able to even come close to beating the best American players. Seve certainly managed to get his twelve teammates into shape and give them the confidence to believe they could win. The evening after the victory, Seve revealed he did not want the captaincy for next year's event. "I'll just be there as a player," he declared. Seve, then aged 42, hoped to be able to add points to his fantastic score of 22.5 points in eight events.

An Inner Strength Greater than His Body

Severiano has always been considered to be the player with the greatest amount of "heart," a man with all the inner reserves of energy which are needed to become a

THE CAPTAIN MAKING HIS SELECTION

(Facing) *Twelve great names left no room for Miguel Angel Martin.*

champion. His mental and physical energy conceal an Achilles' heel, however. Since 1977, Ballesteros has been suffering from severe back pain. This is the result, no doubt, of his endless hours of practice and the violent swings he uses to send the ball as far as possible. Thirty years of championship golf can take its toll on the spine. Ballesteros knows it, but the flame of ambition still burns brightly within him. "I'm still waiting to win the U.S. Open and the U.S. PGA, and why not a third Masters?" Seve is a devoted father and loves going home to his family in Pedrena. Will he manage to combine all the ingredients needed for lasting success? Only the future will tell if he has the physical strength.

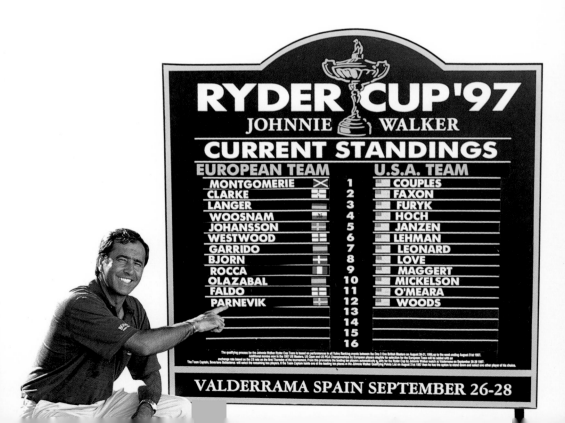

Tom Kite

TOM KITE

BORN DECEMBER 9, 1949
IN AUSTIN, TEXAS

MARRIED, 3 CHILDREN

1 MAJOR
U.S. OPEN 1992

22 PRO WINS

RYDER CUP
1979-81-83-85-87-89-93

CAPTAIN IN 1997

LIVES IN AUSTIN, TEXAS

The peak of Tom Kite's career to date is undoubtedly his captaincy of the Ryder Cup team in 1997; he has been one of the finest golfers for two decades. Tom began playing when he was only six and won his first tournament at the age of eleven. He was a childhood playmate of Ben Crenshaw in Texas, and was raised by one of golf's great mentors, Harvey Penick. This famous teacher was faced with contrasting personalities in the pair of champions he was creating: one of them adored practice and the other preferred to play a real round of golf. Kite had a rather timid, concentrated, and studious nature, and thus enjoyed training and practicing for hours. Penick would say later that while every golfer has the makings of a champion, "they like to train their strength while they ought to be doing the opposite."

Kite is a perfectionist, just like another famous Texan—Ben Hogan. He works regular hours on his game, which has given him exceptional consistency. He knows how to limit the length of his drive, unlike Miller, and concentrates on his short game. What he loses in length he gains in his mastery of the pitching-wedge and sand-wedge, in which his technique is irreproachable on any shot of less than one hundred yards. This skill has made him an example to all golfers and turned him into a redoubtable player in match play; in his Ryder Cup performance, he has scored 17 points in seven meets.

The Best Players Never to Have Won a Major

Despite his skill, Kite was unable to win a major tournament for a significant part of his career. His well-deserved break finally came in 1992 at the U.S. Open at Pebble Beach. On the last afternoon a storm blew up from the ocean. Thanks to his brilliant mastery of the game, Tom managed to shoot par despite the fierce winds, and his putting was devastating. Neither Jeff Sluman nor Colin Montgomerie were able to stand in the way of his dream that afternoon. Kite richly deserved that Major, having come in second three times in the Masters and once in the British Open. He took a shot at the British Open in 1985 and at the U.S. Open in 1989. Victory was within his grasp, only to be snatched away in the end.

TOM KITE

(Page 67) *The quiet strength of the American circuit.*

THE NINTH HOLE AT PEBBLE BEACH

(Preceding pages) *His whole career was saved by his victory in the U.S. Open in 1992.*

RYDER CUP CAPTAIN IN 1997

Mark O'Meara and Tiger Woods, two of the players in his armada.

A Remarkable Ryder Cup Record

Kite has scored 17 points for his team, taking a lot of scalps in the singles play on the last days of the tournament. Of the seven meets in which he has played (1979, '81, '83, '85, '87, '89, '93), Tom has beaten Langer (1993), Lyle (1981 and 1987), Jacklin (1979), and Clark (1989). Only Ballesteros and Torrance managed to draw their matches against the man who has never lost a singles match. The only players on the U.S. Ryder Cup team with records to match Kite's have been Billy Casper, Gene Littler, Lee Trevino, Lanny Wadkins, Arnold Palmer, and Jack Nicklaus.

1997 Ryder Cup Captain

Kite was appointed U.S. captain of the 1997 Ryder Cup in which he was matched against Ballesteros, the European captain. The chosen course, Valderrama in Spain, is rather narrow and does not suit the long shots of Woods, Love, and Couples. Kite arranged a recce of the course in late June, before the British Open at Troon. Only three players took the trouble to go. The American team looked so much better on paper that most of the players underestimated the necessity of Kite's strategy. Three months later, Europe won by one point, despite the fact that the U.S. team contained so many outstanding winners of Majors: Tiger Woods (Masters), Justin Leonard (British), and Davis Love III (U.S. PGA). Experience of the course made all the difference.

AN INSEPARABLE TRIO

Harvey Penick between Kite and Crenshaw, his most famous students.

Some sportswriters condemned Kite's style as being less aggressive than his European counterparts, but the players admitted that the Europeans had simply outplayed and outputted them. They agreed that Kite had nothing to regret, either in the selection of players or the order of play. The game was lost in the doubles, where European experience made all the difference. The 1999 Ryder Cup captain was appointed soon afterward—Ben Crenshaw! The fate of the two Texans was once again inexorably entwined.

A Quiet Man who Should Never Be Underestimated

If any player has been proof that consistency is the mother of all wisdom on the Tour, that player is Tom Kite. Without leading in the most representative statistics, Kite is right behind Norman in terms of prize-money won on the Tour. He has pocketed $10 million in his twenty-five-year career, which began when he turned pro in 1972—an amazing feat! From 1981 through 1994, he won at least $200,000 a year (a record for those years). As recently as April 1997, Thomas Oliver Kite, at forty-seven years of age, finished second in the Masters behind the tornado Tiger Woods!

1995 MASTERS, AUGUSTA, THE 18TH GREEN
Victory, tears, and the memory of Penick.

BEN CRENSHAW

Crenshaw is considered to be one of the best putters in the world, as shown by his two extraordinary wins in the 1984 and 1995 Masters. What a lesson in ability to understand the contours of the green! His uncontrollable show of emotion on the 18th green in Augusta in 1995 remains one of golf's greatest moments. His mentor, Harvey Penick, had died only a couple of days earlier. This golfing guru had coached Crenshaw and Kite in their teenage years, and as a result they became university golf champions with their NCAA wins in 1971, '72, and '73. After the 1997 season, the two men each scored 19 victories in their career.

Crenshaw's record does not match Kite's in terms of the Ryder Cup. He has only managed to score 3.5 points in four of the Cups in comparison with Kite's 17 points in seven events. Crenshaw went down in history when he broke his famous putter, Little Ben, in a fit of pique at the sixth hole of the 1987 Ryder Cup. He had to continue with his one-iron and lost the match. The Europeans won 15-13, their first victory on American soil.

Although Crenshaw is three years younger than Kite, he won his first Major eight years earlier. Ben twice came in second in the British Open in the late 1970s. Crenshaw has a passion for history and for old golfing equipment. He has also taken up golf course design; Crenshaw is following in the footsteps of George Fazio, Palmer, Nicklaus, Weiskopf, and McCumber.

AN INCOMPARABLE PUTTER
St. Andrews, 1995 British Open, the road hole bunker at the 17th.

GREG NORMAN

The man now nicknamed the Great White Shark was originally dubbed the Golden Bear, or Norman the Little Bear, by the Australian press. Ever since he discovered Nicklaus's book on golf he has idolized the original Golden Bear. As a teenager in Brisbane, Greg thought of golf as a ladies' game. His mother, who had a three handicap, sometimes used to let him caddie for her. He enjoyed talking strategy with her, but preferred faster, more physical sports. At the age of eighteen, however, he began to throw all of his famous energy into the game of golf. From then on, the boy who dreamed of becoming a fighter pilot had his feet firmly on the ground, and he began to show promise with the amazing length of his drive.

Jack Nicklaus Becomes his Role Model

Greg began poring over his mother's golf manuals. In just two years, Norman reduced his handicap from 27 to scratch. He also developed a passion for game strategy. The two great Australian champions, Peter Thomson and Ken Nagle, have claimed that the courses on which they practiced prepared them well for the European and American Tours. Norman never concealed his admiration for Nicklaus. He was fascinated by his power and intelligence. He took the advice of the

WITH JACK NICKLAUS
The Golden Bear inspired the Great White Shark.

great man, determined to pursue a career which would emulate that of his idol as closely as possible.

Practice at the Royal Queensland

"It was perfectly obvious that this young man was going to succeed in whatever he chose to do; he was driven by an amazing self-confidence. But I still can't get over what he's managed to achieve, it has been remarkable," explains his then-coach, Charlie Earp, the Royal Queensland Golf Club's resident pro. Greg turned professional in 1976 and won the West Lake Classic in his fourth competition on the Australian Tour. He played on the European Tour for six seasons until 1982, when he won three consecutive victories and placed at the top in the Order of Merit. By then he felt ready to accept Nicklaus's invitation to accompany him on the American tour. Meanwhile,

NORMAN HAS ALWAYS DEALT WITH ADVERSITY HEAD-ON...
He has never run away from trouble.

THE 1993 U.S. PGA IS OUT OF REACH

So close to his first U.S. Major, at Inverness, Ohio.

the victory-hungry Norman continued to play all over the world, including Hong Kong, Australia, Japan, France, Sweden, and the British Isles. In 1984, Norman took the plunge and entered the U.S. Tour. He won his two first victories, the Kemper Open and the Canadian Open.

Norman Turns Himself into an Industry

In the 1980s, thanks to Mark McCormack's IMG company, Norman started a hugely profitable business, endorsing products from beer cans to golfing equipment. In the 1990s, he began demanding guaranteed payments of up to $300,000 per tournament, just for showing up. He soon became involved in golf architecture, and in the early 1990s showed an interest in the World Tour. He signed an agreement for TV rights with that other well-known Australian shark, Rupert Murdoch, and set up the first World Tour in 1994. The PGA Tour refused to allow Norman's company to televise their matches. In 1997 they developed their own plan, and combined with the five major Tours. PGA Tour director, Tim Finchem, thus gained control of world golf and the television rights to golf, which he had denied to Norman!

Two Victories and Eight Second Places in the Majors

Norman was lucky in two British Opens and did exceptionally well in the Grand Slam heats. His six-stroke victory at Turnberry in 1986 is a clear demonstration of his

NOT LOST FOR EVERYONE

Bob Tway wins the U.S. PGA in 1986, benefiting from Norman's collapse at the last hole.

abilities. Norman admits, however, that on the eve of the last tournament, Nicklaus had drawn his attention to the pressure of his grip. "You have to watch out for the pressure of your hands on the handle before each stroke and be careful not to hold on too tight," was his advice. Jack, who had recently won his sixth Masters, did not want to see the player whom he felt so closely resembled him miss big opportunities for winning. Greg was expected to do well in the 1984 Majors, especially in the U.S. Open, but he was soundly thrashed in the play-off by Fuzzy Zoeller. Nevertheless, the Australian was a formidable player in each match in the Grand Slam. Greg Norman was in the lead by the end of the third round of each Major in 1986. In April 1986, in the Masters, he used a four-iron on his approach to the 18th green, but the shot went right and he had to concede victory to the Golden Bear. A month after Norman's win in Turnberry, Bob Tway sunk a bunker shot to defeat him.

So Close to Victory in Several Majors

As luck would have it, victory was snatched from Norman again the following year, when Larry Mize holed a chip-shot to win the 1987 Masters. Greg berated himself for failing to sink the putt at the 18th, which would have guaranteed him victory. There was a sequel. In 1989 at Troon, Greg produced a final-day scorecard of 64. He forced the play-off with Calcavecchia and Grady, two Australians against one American. On the last hole, Norman took out his driver to play this par-four hole. Several

GREG NORMAN

BORN FEBRUARY 10, 1955
IN QUEENSLAND, AUSTRALIA

MARRIED, 2 CHILDREN

2 MAJORS
BRITISH OPEN 1986-93

71 PRO WINS

LIVES IN HOBE SOUND, FLA.

spectators speculated as to why the Great White Shark had chosen this club. As expected, the shot went wide of the mark and ended up in a sand trap.

Undisputed Leader in the Art of Money-Making

In 1993, Norman walked away with the British Open, beating Nick Faldo on the very demanding Royal St. George's course at Sandwich, Kent, in southern England. Norman's numerous victories on every continent were making him golf's wealthiest player. At the end of the 1997 season, Norman ranked top overall in the United States in terms of prize-money, with nearly $12 million to his credit over his eighteen-year career. Jack Nicklaus ranks 27th in the same field, despite more wins, but times have changed and there is far more money to be won today. One thing is clear, Norman would be happy to exchange a few million just to be able to claim a title or two in the American Majors. He came so close to winning Augusta's coveted Green Jacket that he wanted to erase the cruel memory of the 1996 Masters.

Starting Afresh after April 1996

Nineteen ninety-five was a good year for Greg in the United States. He finished second in the U.S. Open and third in the

RELIEF

When the ball disappears over the horizon in the direction of the green.

A TRUE ATHLETE

He has exceptional power and energy.

Masters, and was looking forward to the first match in the Grand Slam in 1996. He was in peak condition, and he won the Doral-Ryder Open for the third time, setting a course record with a four-day total of 265. His scores of 67-69-67-66 were proof that the Great White Shark was in great shape. At Augusta, he started strongly, equaling the course record by posting a 63. In the second round, Greg stayed in the lead at 12 under par, and by the end of the third day he was six strokes ahead of Nick Faldo. Unfortunately, disaster struck on the back nine. The Englishman caught up with Norman, whose game collapsed in front of millions. It was the last thing on earth that Bob Jones would have wanted to happen on the tournament course that bears his name. The physical strength, confidence, and determination of the Australian melted away. After what had happened to Ben Crenshaw in 1995, everyone at the 18th green in Augusta was stunned.

ON THE GREEN

(Preceding pages) *He casts his shadow over many tournaments.*

A PASSION FOR SPEED

Ferraris, helicopters, jets…off the course, Norman loves to indulge his appetite for risk-taking.

Trying to Forget

Greg went off to recharge his batteries with his family and with Jack Nicklaus, who was living nearby in Florida. It had been a hard knock for Norman and it brought back unhappy memories. He could only comfort himself with the thought that great golfers in the past had suffered similar experiences. The great challenge Norman faces is the breaking of the spell that seems to haunt his play-offs or his final putts. The Great White Shark cannot cope with that kind of pressure, as was proven again in the Australian Open in late 1997, when he was unable to seize his chance against Lee Westwood. Again, Norman was haunted by his past and his putt went off the mark. Whenever this kind of thing happens, Norman takes out his frustration by piloting his private jet. Speed and fishing are two important elements in the life of this predator, who earned his nickname in these pursuits. Speed means a lot to him, as evidenced by two helicopters, a jet plane, five speedboats, two jet-skis, seven Ferraris, and two Rolls Royces (license plates: Aussie 1 and Aussie 2). The need to take risks is something he shares with his father, who also served in the Royal Australian Air Force; however, that's one of the few things he shares with Norman, Sr. The two men have little contact. Some psychologists would interpret Norman's career as a perpetual quest to please his father. According to Greg's mother, father and son are very much alike. Greg quit IMG and Frank Williams became his manager. Norman is "too much at times"; his Terminator-style behavior is hard for his family and friends to deal with. Norman married in 1981; his daughter, Morgan-Leigh, was born in 1982 and his son, Gregory junior in 1985.

FALDO

NICK

EXTRICATING HIMSELF FROM A BUNKER

This is one of the specialities of this past master of the short game.

Nick Faldo was certainly the best golfer in the world in the 1980s and early 1990s. His performance in the Majors was outstanding. In order to reach these heights, Nick had to work hard on his swing and change it radically. He was not happy with the way he moved under pressure. Since he is tall, the energetic movement of his body and legs too often altered the plane of his swing, affecting his stability and consistency.

David Leadbetter's Student

David Leadbetter, who comes from Zimbabwe, is a pro European Tour veteran who now devotes himself to teaching technique to the best players. David's mechanical concept of the swing was designed to bring Faldo the consistency he needed. The job was long and hard and required Faldo to completely change the way he moved. The lower half of his body had to be a stationary block of resistance in order to propel the upper part of the body and the arms to move in the same plane. For two years,

HAVING A BALL

(Previous page) Doesn't he bear a resemblance to Jimmy Connors, James Bond, or Harrison Ford?

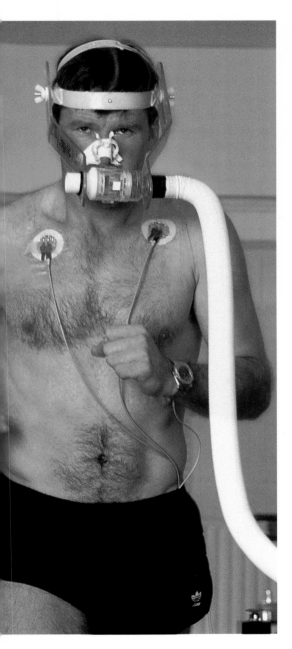

starting in 1986, Nick worked hard and finally managed to bring the action of his left elbow into harmony with the action of his legs. While Faldo did not gain length on his shots, he gained much in consistency. Faldo's success in 1992 helped Leadbetter shoot to the top. He created his own golfing school based at Lake Nona, Florida, and set up schools in other countries, including France, England, Austria, and Germany. His most famous students were Johansson, Price, McNulty, and Frost. Not all of them stayed and not all of them succeeded, as was the case with Bob Tway and Howard Clark.

A Gifted Young Sportsman

As a teenager, the young Faldo had enjoyed competitive sports such as cycling or swimming. He became interested in golf at age 14, when he watched Jack Nicklaus in the Masters. When Faldo finally opted for golf, the "Golden Bear" became the player he most wanted to emulate in his quest to become a champion golfer. His parents, who had always given their son whatever he wanted, were very supportive of his ambitions. Three years later, Nick joined the national junior team together with

UNDER SUPERVISION
A more demanding sportsman than he looks.

WHERE'S THE FLAG GONE?

Looking for the flag from the rough is like looking for a needle…

Sandy Lyle, who was to become his most consistent opponent in his amateur years. In 1975 he won the British Amateur Championship at the age of only 17. Opponents, but never enemies, Faldo and Lyle went off together to the selection examinations for the University of Houston. Lyle failed; although Nick passed, he quit school a few weeks later, feeling he would not get enough time to devote to golf.

Faldo Turns Pro in 1976

The early years were tough but quite lucrative for a young man of 20. He won his first significant victory in 1978 at the PGA Colgate Championship, which put him in third place in the Order of Merit. Faldo was still overshadowed by Ballesteros and Lyle, the leading Europeans in those years. Nothing much had happened in professional British golf since the exploits of Tony Jacklin ten years earlier. Lyle and Faldo represented the hope of reviving the golfing luster 50 years after Henry Cotton. Nineteen

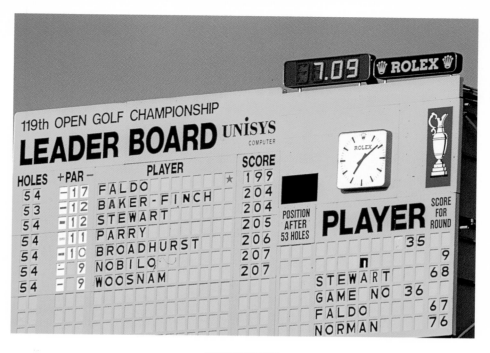

1990 BRITISH OPEN

At Muirfield, Faldo was in the lead until the 72nd hole.

eighty-three was far and away Faldo's best year as a professional, with four wins, three of them in playoffs. For the first time he topped the annual rankings. Faldo left for the United States in 1984, and immediately won the Sea Pines Heritage Classic. Overall, his winnings in the Grand Slam were meager, as he only finished sixth in the British Open.

A Difficult Relationship with the Press

Faldo is not a public person; he doesn't enjoy talking to the press and hates the critics. He exhibits some of the character traits of the spoiled child, which have aroused the antipathy of certain journalists. He has even been nicknamed "El Foldo," the loser. His divorce from his wife Melanie added fuel to the flames. Faldo had started seeing Gill, the secretary who worked for his manager, Mark McCormack, and the press went wild when he registered at a hotel in Hawaii while passing Gill off as his wife. Faldo never really regained the unconditional support of the media

1995 SCOTTISH OPEN

Faldo, Montgomerie, and one of the newer great British golfers, Gordon Sherry.

after that—especially the British press. His character makes him more appreciated as a sportsman than as a man. In the late 1990s, the press started to view the champion a little more objectively and finally stopped prying into his private life, keeping their distance during his second divorce in 1997.

The Race for the Majors

His longtime adversary Sandy Lyle was the first to win a Major. It was during this period that Faldo chose Leadbetter to help him remodel his swing. A victory in the Spanish Open restored his confidence after three years in the wilderness. He went on to win his first Grand Slam Title in the 1987 British Open on the difficult Muirfield course. Faldo has always had an amazing rhythm—he does not hit the ball, he sweeps it up. At Muirfield, with a one-iron in his hands, he withstood the repeated onslaught of Craig Stadler, Roger Davis, and finally the tenacious Paul Azinger.

Faldo played all 18 holes at par and finished the round at five under par, winning the Claret Jug on the final hole with a 4-foot putt on a downward slope. His long shots were reliable; he managed to get out of sand traps with a few memorable shots, and

NICK FALDO

BORN JULY 18, 1957
IN WELWYN GARDEN CITY,
ENGLAND

3 CHILDREN

6 MAJORS
BRITISH OPEN 1987-90-92
MASTERS 1989-90-96

39 PRO WINS

RYDER CUP 1977-79
1981-83-85-87-89-91-93-95-97

LIVES IN ORLANDO, FLA.
AND WEYBRIDGE, ENGLAND

THE MACHINE SHOWS EXCITEMENT, PEBBLE BEACH

A putt sunk at the 18th in the 1992 U.S. Open.

his putting was perfect. From that moment on, he studied his swing from all angles. The way Faldo hits the ball and his slow rhythm have become the classic swing movement which golfers hope to emulate.

The American Majors

Faldo came close to winning the U.S. Open in 1988 when he played Curtis Strange at the Brookline Country Club. Big Nick had the perfect game for the competition. He drives straight down the middle and has a good short game, which helps him avoid troublesome roughs. Except for 1992, when he found himself just behind Nick Price in the U.S. PGA, Faldo has never managed to capture the U.S. Open or the U.S. PGA. Nevertheless, he has won the British Open and the Masters. He won the Green Jacket for the first time in 1989, defeating Scott Hoch in a playoff. In the following year, Nick won a double, again in a playoff, against Ray Floyd and pocketed his third title at Augusta. It was a dramatic day, an occasion remembered more for Greg Norman's collapse over the last nine holes than for the magnificent 67 achieved by Faldo on the last afternoon of the tournament. The two champions share certain characteristics, such as Jack Nicklaus being their inspiration, their solitary nature, athletic build, and the fact that neither has won the U.S. Open or the U.S. PGA.

The Record of Victories in the Ryder Cup

Faldo was first selected in 1977, when he was not yet 20, the youngest player ever to be selected. He played his first match paired with Peter Oosterhuis and they won the match by two and one. Nick won all three of his matches. Later, he and Ian Woosnam made an excellent pair who would also become the most photographed of the British golfers. In 1997, Faldo took part in his eleventh meet and scored a total of 25 points, beating the record of victories held by the American Billy Casper. Nick had a wealth of experience, of which Ballesteros wanted to take full advantage. He selected Faldo again in 1997, deciding to team him with the young Lee Westwood.

Faldo Pursues His Solitary Career in the United States

Faldo eventually decided to leave Mark McCormack's IMG and hired John Simpson to manage him and his finances. He has earned a lot from the various Tours, including

FALDO'S STYLE

Technique, precision, rhythm, balance.

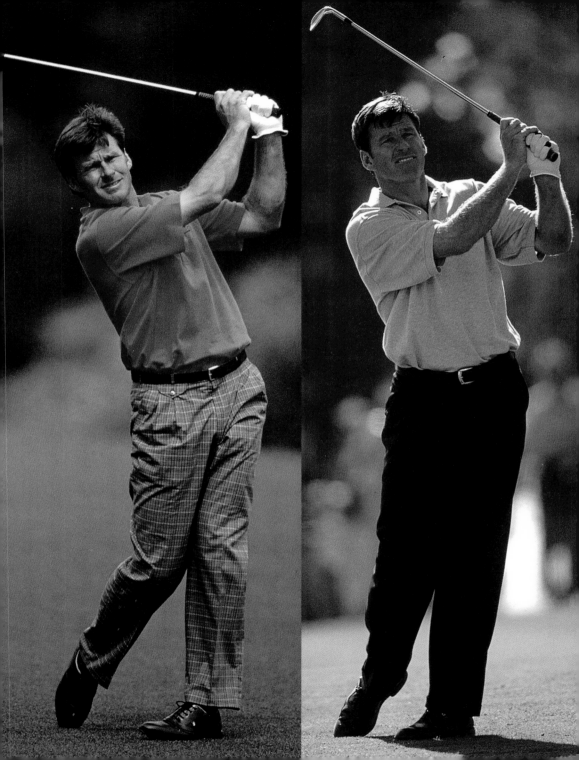

more than five million pounds in Europe and four million dollars in the United States. IMG had contributed to his finances by arranging endorsements and other paid activities. Pringle and Mizuno are some of the trademarks that have helped Faldo indulge his passion for helicopters, as well as for fishing—a sport he shares with others on the U.S. Tour.

Muirfield and St. Andrews

Faldo proved his flair in the early 1990s by brilliantly winning the British Open at St. Andrews (1990) then at Muirfield (1992), courses that bring out the best in players. Nick demonstrated a range of shots each more accurate than the last. Payne Stewart, Mark McNulty, and John Cook have born the brunt of Faldo's success. His consistency, his game plan, and his analysis make him a number-one favorite in all the Majors. Efficiency rather than panache are typical of the British champion.

Since 1995, Faldo has preferred to play in the American Tour because he appreciates the American courses and the general lifestyle. However, apart from the three Green

1997 RYDER CUP

The greatest number of wins and mentor to young Lee Westwood.

FALDO AND WOOSNAM: THE MOST PHOTOGRAPHED PAIR

(Facing) *Two very different physiques, maximum efficiency.*

Jackets he has worn in the Masters, he has not been that prolific in terms of victories. By the end of 1997, he had won only three other trophies in the United States. Having devoted so much energy to improving his swing, Nick Faldo has tended to neglect his putting. This has taken its toll. His confidence has been damaged over the years, returning only sporadically, and only when he is winning.

Putting will become the key to Faldo's career in his later years. He still has a few dreams to come true, such as winning the U.S. Open and the U.S. PGA.

WINNER OF THE U.S. MASTERS IN 1996

Faldo has worn the Green Jacket three times.

WITH FANNY SUNNESON

(Facing) *His secret garden: designing greens and golf courses.*

NICK

PRICE

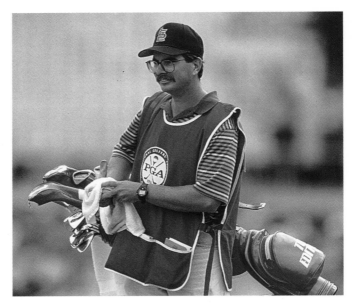

JEFF "SQUEEKY" MEDLEN

Price's friend and caddy.

For three years (1992–1994) Price was the greatest player in the world. Yet those glory years can never erase the tragic death of his best friend and caddy Jeff "Squeeky" Medlen, who died of leukemia in June 1997. The illness had set in a year before, and came as a terrible shock for both of them. Price and Squeeky had never had the regular pro-caddie relationship. On the contrary, they were true friends who went through great joy and sadness together. When he learned of Jeff's illness, Nick pledged that he would do all he could to provide the necessary support, both medical and financial. In 1997, at the age of 40, Price decided to change his priorities. He hired a manager to look after his business affairs, so as to have more time to spend with his family and to play the game. "I feel that at my age I must continue to play and train. I don't have to stay in an office to manage my business. I have to be with my family or else doing some training, or be out on the course. The loss of Squeeky has made me stop and concentrate on the essential things in life."

AT AUGUSTA IN 1994

(Preceding page) *The Masters: a Major he would love to win.*

Medlen Lends a Hand to John Daly

Nick Price had a few health problems himself in late 1991 and when Sue, his wife, was about to give birth, Price decided not to play in the U.S. PGA. John Daly was brought in as ninth reserve and arrived without a caddie. Jeff Medlen was available and they decided to team up. The task was not easy; Daly was unknown on the Tour and the length of his drive was rather disconcerting. Amazingly, the two men worked well together and Daly brought home his first Major. He gave all the credit to Squeeky who, in the four rounds, gave him the benefit of all his experience. The following year, it was Price's turn to receive Medlen's advice. The caddy had experienced the pressure of the U.S. PGA and he passed it on to the Zimbabwean player. Price's victory at the U.S. PGA was no fluke. Nick already had eleven wins under his belt. After a few years spent in Africa (1977–1980), Price left for Europe where success came quite almost immediately in the 1980 Canon European Masters.

Price Attracts Attention in Troon in 1982

The British Open had always inspired Nick, who had the upper hand on the course in Troon in 1992. It was the first time he was center stage in the Grand Slam. Tom Watson, the more experienced player, dealt him a death-blow, costing Price the win, and allowing Peter Oosterhuis to catch up with him. His subsequent attempts at the Majors were less spectacular, and at the U.S. PGA he finished fifth. Price did better during the 1987 British Open at Muirfield, but could not compete with the Faldo-Azinger duo when they fought it out over the last holes.

In the following year at the Royal Lytham St. Anne's, Nick took the lead and seemed set for victory at last—but he hadn't figured on Ballesteros, who beat him on the last hole with a near-perfect approach shot. Nick decided to consult sports psychologist Bob Rotella, who taught him how to think straight out on the course, especially in tricky situations, and not to dwell on poor shots and missed opportunities.

A Career on the Rise

The work Price began with Rotella soon began to pay off. In the 1990 season, Price asked Squeeky to become his caddie. Watson had also made him an offer, but Squeeky preferred Price. Price doubled his wins on the American Tour, finishing six times in

IN THE 1982 BRITISH OPEN AT TROON

Only the great Tom Watson could deny Price a win in this Major.

HISTORY REPEATS ITSELF

In the 1988 British Open, at Lytham, Ballesteros snatched victory from him.

the top ten. This winning streak bore fruit in 1991. Nick won the Byron Nelson Classic in May, followed by the Canadian Open a few days before the birth of his son, Gregory. Nick and his wife Sue have had two more children, Robyn Frances in 1993 and Kimberly Rae three years later. Early in the season, Nick was full of confidence and ended in sixth place in the Masters. Medlen and Price worked brilliantly together, and victory in the U.S. PGA at Bellerive in August 1992 crowned a fruitful 15-year career. But Price did not feel he had "arrived" until he finished three-up on the likes of Gene Sauers, Nick Faldo, John Cook, and Jim Gallagher.

Price Beats Faldo and Norman

Becoming the world's best player when Nick Faldo and Greg Norman are also contenders is a significant achievement. And there were a few young lions with sharp teeth who were in great shape, such as Corey Pavin, John Cook, and Paul Azinger. Nevertheless, Nick was more than a match for them and ended the season at the top of the Order of Merit with record winnings of nearly $1.5 million a year. Price had no fewer than six wins in 1993. He did even better in the following year, with eight wins, six of them in the United States, and two Majors in a row in a single season. Nineteen ninety-four was also a fantastic year for Price. No one had enjoyed a season like that since Tom Watson in 1982. Nick had become a complete master of his art, doing so without becoming arrogant, which gained him tremendous respect. Pavin would say of Price's victory in the U.S. PGA: "We soon realized that we were all playing for second place. Nick made us understand that he was unbeatable when he took the lead, ending six strokes ahead. He walked away with the tournament."

Price Finally Wins the British Open

On his fifteenth attempt, with the benefit of more experience, Price was finally awarded the coveted Claret Jug, which had eluded him in 1982 and 1988 (Watson and Ballesteros together had deprived him of this Major). At Turnberry in 1994, Jesper Parnevik took the lead in the British Open with just a few holes left to play. Nick went on the offensive, producing an extraordinary shot at the 16th, a difficult par four with a green protected by a stream. Nick birdied, but still found himself two shots behind. The 17th was a par five that Price managed to play in three shots, including an incredibly long putt—for an Eagle!

AT HIS PEAK

Mark McNulty congratulates Nick in Sun City, 1993.

"His life, experience, and intellectual honesty will make him the perfect president of world golf . . . if the job were ever created."

AT LAST, WINNER OF THE BRITISH OPEN

He surprised Jesper Parnevik at Turnberry in 1994.

Parnevik had produced an unnecessary bogey on the final hole. Price realized that a par would win it and he reached the center of the green with his second shot. When two putts handed him the victory with one shot to spare, he knew he had chosen the right career.

The Best Player in the World Has a Spell of Bad Luck

The next three seasons were difficult due to Price's personal health problems (mainly sinusitis and back pains) and those of his great friend Jeff Medlen. After 15 months without a win, Price was once again victorious in early 1997 on the European Tour, the Dimension Data, and the South African PGA Championship. June was a very dark month with Squeeky's death at the age of 43. Nick determined to focus on his essential goals and work to maintain his lead in the world golfing scene. "I'll win again," he claimed at the end of the season.

Price is considered one of the most balanced personalities on the Tour, and his natural inner strength also makes him a man of principle. Because he is so well respected, he can say out loud what everyone else only dares to think. At the last British Open at Troon, some players were playing such a slow game that it became unbearable to him. Nick said to Faldo and Langer: "Eighteen holes ought to be played in less than four hours, not more than five." Few players would dare to be so blunt, but Price believes that if he speaks out, golf can only benefit. In this, he has joined the ranks of Jack Nicklaus, Bobby Jones, Arnold Palmer, and Henry Cotton.

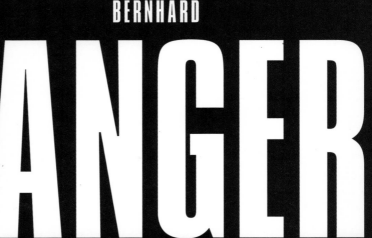

BERNHARD
LANGER

WITH HIS CADDY PETER COLEMAN

A twosome who have faced every challenge together.

The name Bernhard means "bear heart" in German. In 1957, Langer's parents chose this name for their son in the hope that he would be as brave as a bear, and indeed Langer hasn't disappointed their expectations. Bernhard spends hours on the putting green, determined to solve his putting difficulties. He is not the first golfer forced to tackle this problem; his predecessors have included Vardon, Snead, and even Hogan.

Langer: A Very Young Victim of Yips

When Langer was only 20, his opponents were remarking on his weakness on the greens. His hands did not seem to want to obey his head. The problem lies in the numbing of nerve endings in his fingers which means he cannot control the club during putts. Yips is a phenomenon that tends to strike older players or those who have spent too much time practicing.

THE 18TH GREEN AT THE BRITISH OPEN 1993

So close to Greg Norman at Royal St. George's.

ALWAYS THE SAME SINCE 1985

Only his attitudes to putting have changed over time.

Langer would seem to be much too young to suffer from this ailment, but then again, he has been playing for a long time. He caddied at the Bavaria Club in Augsburg at the age of 12, and in summer he would pitch a tent on the course and play from sunrise to sunset. The teenager spent his leisure time working for the club members and decided when he was 15 to turn pro, becoming an assistant to the pro, Hans Fehring. Four years later, in 1976, Bernhard timidly entered the Tour.

Four Years Waiting for the First Win

Nineteen seventy-nine and 1980 were great years for Sandy Lyle, the powerful and relaxed Scotsman. He carved out a solid amateur career for himself. Langer's career was still developing, especially since he was drafted into the Luftwaffe, the German air force, for 15 months in 1977. Upon his return to the Tour, he won the Cacharel before turning 25 (he was 17 strokes ahead of his nearest rival). Ballesteros became interested in the young player and in 1979, he was selected for the Ryder Cup team. He offered some basic advice to Bernhard about his putting: "On fast greens you need to use a putter with a heavy head. Your hands will find it easier and they are more accurate when they can clearly feel the head of the club." With this advice, Langer began to regain confidence and won several tournaments, heading the Order of Merit at the end of the 1981 season.

Never Change a Winning Team

Langer arrived alone on the European Tour and did not benefit from referrals from other German pros. He was confident in the small team he formed around him. Willy Hoffmann took care of Langer's swing, often accompanying him to practices for the big tournaments in order to give him a few points of technical advice. Langer's caddy Peter Coleman contributed the experience the young German lacked. This trio was later joined by Vicky, whom Bernhard married in 1984. Their children—Jackie (1986), Stefan (1990), and Christina (1993)—complete the picture, though the presence of faith should not be overlooked. Langer is a devout Christian whose faith is deeply important to him; he holds Bible studies on the Tour with fellow players Corey Pavin, Tom Lehman, and Gavin Levenson.

Faith, One Way of Coping With Pressure

Langer admits that his fate is in God's hands and his arms are subject to divine guidance. Believing that someone else is making the decisions makes it possible to overcome the strain on his nerves, since he believes that everything is predestined. "He has showered me with gifts both in my profession and in my family." Financially, also: this son of a stonemason has already managed to amass $15 million on the Tours.

A TAYLOR-MADE PUTTER

(Following pages) *His abnormally long grip is adapted to his special way of holding the club.*

BERNHARD LANGER

BORN AUGUST 27, 1957
IN ANHAUSEN, GERMANY

MARRIED, 3 CHILDREN

2 MAJORS
MASTERS 1985-93

51 PRO WINS

RYDER CUP
1981-83-85-87-89-91-93-95-97

LIVES IN ANHAUSEN,
GERMANY

In Germany, thanks to IMG and to his brother Erwin, he has launched a huge golfing industry, which includes the construction of courses, management of real estate developments, and organization of tournaments. As in the case of Nicklaus, Faldo, or Norman, Langer's career has been taken over by Mark McCormack and his company, IMG. This "joint venture" opened up the huge German market which caught the golf fever that swept continental Europe in the mid-1980s. Today, as then, Langer is as popular as Franz Beckenbauer, Karl Heinz Rummenige, Boris Becker, or Michael Stich.

Europe's Answer to Tom Kite

Langer knows his weakness and has devoted all his energies to improving his putting. Ever since he was nine years old, he has loved practice and spends whole days training. Bernhard understands that the better his approach shots, the less need he will have for his putter. Like Tom Kite, Langer will become known for shots of less than 100 yards. The pitching- and sand-wedges become weapons of rare precision in his hands. Sand-trap shots are easier for him than a six-foot putt. The resemblance to his contemporary, Tom Kite, is striking. The players share a legendary consistency. Their swings are compact and repetitive, their long irons are remarkable, and their short games show no weakness. Kite and Langer also share an amazing record of wins on the Tour. Each of them ranks second: the German behind Colin Montgomerie and the American behind Greg Norman.

THE FAMILY

One of the basic values that keeps him balanced.

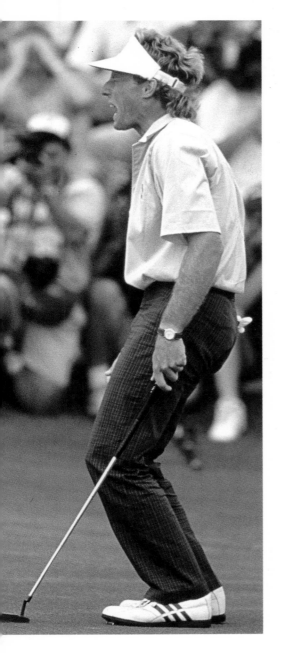

1991 Ryder Cup, Kiawah Island.

The Masters

After his disappointing performance in the British Open against Ballesteros, in 1985 Langer played some of the best golf of his career, dominating the Augusta greens and beating his friend Severiano. Curtis Strange lost his fight with the 13th hole and Rae's Creek to leave the way open for Langer. Ironically, it was the best putter in the world who had to present the Green Jacket to the German. Aware of Langer's profile, Ben Crenshaw sincerely congratulated Bernhard for the feat he had accomplished. Once again, the Bavarian had been able to rely on his team, consisting of Coleman, Hoffmann, and his wife, Vicky. Langer also owes a great deal to Ballesteros. Sandy Lyle, Nick Faldo, Ian Woosnam, and, later, José-Maria Olazábal, followed in the footsteps of those two giants of European golf, Ballesteros and Langer. Eight years later, Langer fought off Chip Beck to win his second Green Jacket. This victory was revenge for his defeat by Beck in the 1989 Ryder Cup.

The Ryder Cup

Langer certainly left an image for posterity when he lost to Hale Irwin in Kiawah Island in 1991 and victory went to the Americans. In the final match, there was only one point between the teams (a replay of the situation in 1989 at the Belfry); one point off the Europeans' possibility of retaining the cup, which had been in their possession since their first victory on American soil in 1987 at Muirfield Village, Ohio.

Langer has not missed any of the nine Ryder Cup matches since 1981 and has won five-and-a-half points in singles matches alone. He has a total of 18 matches won, 15 lost, and five drawn to his credit. Together with Faldo and Ballesteros, Langer is one of the key players on the European team. Now in his forties, Langer appears to be much fresher than others of his generation, such as Woosnam, Lyle, Torrance, Clark, or Feherty.

Did You Say Consistency?

From the Italian Open in 1991, Langer has played 68 competitions without once missing the cut, and that remains a record. If anyone is still not convinced of his talents, Bernhard won four events on the European Tour in the year he turned 40:

ECSTASY

1987 Ryder Cup: the winning shot.

the Italian Open, the Benson and Hedges, the Chemapol Open in the Czech Republic, and the German Masters. In this last tournament, the German broke 60, which was 12 under par! Eleven birdies, an eagle, and a bogey (three putts) became a new record for the Berliner Golf Club. This was Langer's third win, and he did so immediately after the Ryder Cup. He won the German Masters in 1991 right after Kiawah Island and the European Masters after Oak Hill in 1995. With two Green Jackets in his wardrobe and a scorecard of 60 in his fortieth year, Langer can savor the fact that his has been one of the greatest European golfing careers. His intelligence and determination have made him the greatest German golfer of all time.

TRIUMPH

Victory in the 1993 Masters.

Fred Couples

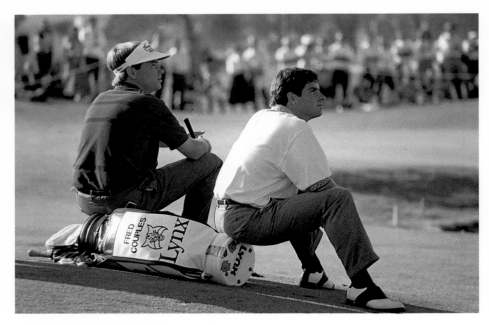

WITH DAVIS LOVE III

A very old friend.

With his "cute kid" looks, Fred has been given two nicknames: "The Big Easy" and "Boom Boom." The second describes the force of his drives, while the first refers to his attitude. Couples, born October 3, 1959, in Seattle, Washington, has an easy-going attitude. This was not popular in Ryder Cup matches; some observers criticized his laid-back behavior, arguing that Fred did not show enough enthusiasm in defending the Stars and Stripes. His friend and mentor, Ray Floyd, who knows him well, has spiritedly defended him: "It's the way he is—Fred plays a relaxed game even if he is intensely nervous. There's no doubt he will give his best to the American team. Don't criticize his attitude—it is sincere and determined." This kind of support helped Fred overcome difficult moments after his defeat at the Belfry against Christy O'Connor.

From Kid to College Grad
Fred discovered the golf course through a friend via a "secret entrance." Not being a club member nor having the money to pay for greens fees, the pair got on the course

(Previous page) *A fine sportsman who has earned his adoring fan club.*

PLAYING IN THE 1992 WORLD CUP

Couples has won this Cup four times.

by sneaking through a hole in the fence. Fred very soon got the feel of game. Much later his father, who worked in the Parks and Leisure Department of the City of Seattle, encouraged him to play more regularly. After doing well as a junior player, Couples enrolled at the University of Houston. Here he met great coaches, Dick Harmon in particular. Dick is the son of Claude Harmon, former winner of the Masters, who also advises Ray Floyd, Lanny Wadkins, Billy Ray Brown, and Steve Elkington. Couples chose the right vehicle for his talent, and was able to turn pro in the fall of 1980.

Rookie of the Year

From his first year, 1981, Fred was noticed, coming second in the Hartford Open behind Hubert Green, who was celebrating the 14th win of his career. Couples won the title of Rookie of the Year. But it took him two years to achieve his first win. In 1983, he won the Kemper Open after a playoff between five players. The following year he won the Tournament Players' Championship. However, he didn't

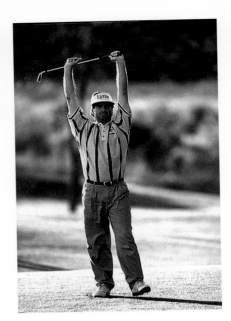 

TYPICAL ATTITUDES

He has always had a need to relax.

play as well he would have liked on the Tour, and once again Harmon came to the rescue, helping him find his balance by advising him to leave more time between tournaments to keep himself fresh for the challenge. Until 1989, Couples had had a steady career without any sensational achievements, though he won the Byron Nelson Classic on one occasion. He was about to experience his best years.

The Early Nineties

In 1990, Fred found himself among the top ten in the Order of Merit. He won another three victories but never found the keys to Major success. In the U.S. PGA, while he was leading on the last round, his putting began to let him down and Fred had to concede victory to Australian Wayne Grady, who had experienced a similar problem in the British Open in 1989. Ray Floyd helped his friend back into the saddle by winning a foursome tournament with him. Ray says of his friend's game: "The length of his drive shows up better in this formula of taking alternate shots (foursomes), because it's great to be able to

ALFRED DUNHILL CUP 1993, ST. ANDREWS

Teeing off at the 18th, a classic stance addressing the ball.

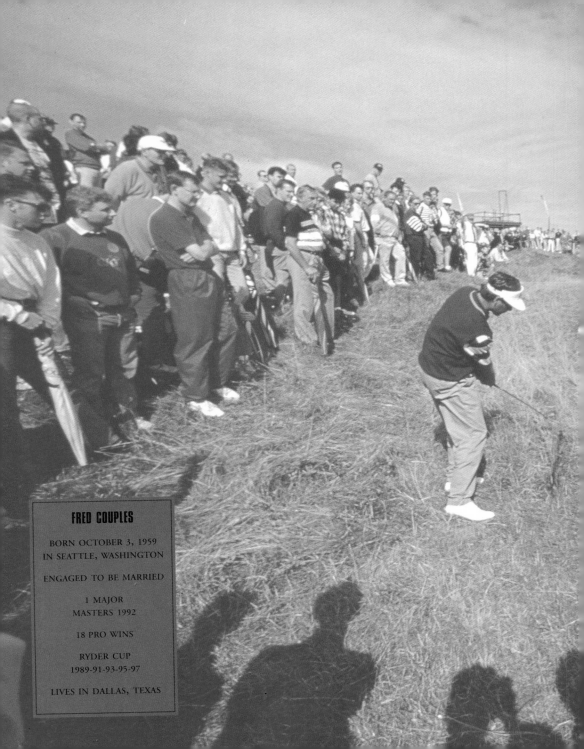

FRED COUPLES

BORN OCTOBER 3, 1959
IN SEATTLE, WASHINGTON

ENGAGED TO BE MARRIED

1 MAJOR
MASTERS 1992

18 PRO WINS

RYDER CUP
1989-91-93-95-97

LIVES IN DALLAS, TEXAS

hit a second shot from his drives—they go so far that it makes the game much easier." Then came 1992, when he won three victories, including the dreamed-of Major. The ghost of Bob Jones seems to have surfaced several times during the Masters. There can be no other explanation for Couples's ball hovering on the edge of the 12th green, when it ought to have dropped to the bottom of the waiting pond.

The 1992 Masters, and the 1989 Ryder Cup Revenge

Couples's Green Jacket was richly deserved. Fred is a breath of fresh air in a sport in which players are becoming rather mechanical. He suffered, however, a major setback at Sutton Coldfield, England, during the 1989 Ryder Cup. In his first doubles match, in which he was paired with Wadkins, Fred lost, not managing a single birdie. Floyd, the American team captain, couldn't have found him a better partner against Clark and James. After Couples confessed to feeling under a lot of pressure during his first match, Ray stopped selecting him to play any matches before the singles. During the singles, Couples was one up after 14 holes but lost to Christy O'Connor, Jr., who caught up with him before the last hole. Then Fred produced a magnificent drive on the difficult 18th hole. The Irishman had been much further back from the green and needed to use a two-iron to make it there. Fred took his eight-iron but missed the target. The rest is history. This was Fred's only singles defeat in the five times he played in the Ryder Cup (1989, '91, '93, '95, and '97).

Back Pains

In late 1994, Couples began to suffer from back pain and had to stop playing for two months. He returned to Europe, winning two events on the European Tour. Once again, Harmon showed good judgment and taught Fred to manage his time so that he would have at least six weeks between competitions. In order to do his best, Couples needs to feel completely fresh, both physically and mentally.

Couples stopped featuring in the Majors, though he had good seasons and was selected for the Ryder Cup. His lower back pain meant he could not handle long training sessions. Yet, financially speaking, 1996 was his best year ever. He won the

BIG HORN, CALIFORNIA, 1995

(Facing) *Under the watchful eye of "Fluff," who was then caddying for Peter Jacobsen.*

ROYAL ST. GEORGE'S, 1993

(Preceding pages) *Couples's game is a big crowd-puller.*

THE FLYING ELBOW

Freedom and smoothness in his inimitable swing.

Tournament Players Championship with a sensational 64 in the last round, bringing his winnings to $1,248,102—almost a million dollars more than in 1995.

Swan Song

Couples's amazing recovery in 1996 masked the insidious back pain problems, which recurred the following year. Early in 1997 he was no longer capable of playing a full year on the circuit. He only participated in 15 tournaments and dropped to 55th place in the Order of Merit. Yet he was selected to play in the 1997 Ryder Cup by Captain Tom Kite, and taught Ian Woosnam a lesson at Valderrama by winning by eight and seven in their third match in a row in six years. If the Big Easy ever left the circuit, all the supporters of this anti-hero would sorely miss the most relaxed swing in the world.

Most Popular Player

Whether he organizes charity matches or pursues his passion for collecting Mustang cars, Fred Couples will always act in a natural and relaxed way, doing his thing in a world that has difficulty understanding him.

Couples has spent one third of his professional life in the Top Ten on the Tour; only Nicklaus and Norman have done better. If his profile is markedly different from the others, he still remains the most popular figure on the circuit. Celebrities including Pete Sampras, Jack Nicholson, and Clint Eastwood helped him to buy the Lynx brand of golfing equipment from the parent company, Black Cat—the group of friends had no problem putting together the $37 million needed. Couples was appointed vice-president of the new corporation. If popularity has anything to do with sales, the investment will prove a profitable one!

Bad Times and Good Times

Fred does not know how long it will be before his back problems end his golf career. Only time will tell, which is also true of the cancer that struck his fiancée. "I told him we met at almost the same time, Fred, me and this damned cancer," she explained. Couples replied with courage and sincerity: "I want to fight it along with her. I blame myself for not having been there enough for my mother, Violet, before she passed away in 1994. My girlfriend has kids, and it's an important experience to have your family around you." In 1997, Tom Couples died from leukemia. Fred canceled all of his competitions for more than a month to stay at the bedside of his 74-year-old father. Now, his family comes before everything else—putts and missed drives are of secondary importance to the Big Easy.

In early 1998, Couples made a comeback. His fiancée, Thais Bren, seemed to be recovering from her cancer. Couples was a changed man. He was in good spirits and, amazingly, won the Bob Hope Chrysler Classic in a playoff. The $414,000 check represented the single largest amount of prize money he had won since his 1996 victory in the Players Championship. "You don't know how much I love golf. What's more, I love competitions, even if it doesn't always show." For this man, life is full of surprises.

ERNIE ELS

Theodore Ernest Els was born in Johannesburg, South Africa, on October 17, 1969. He won a tennis tournament as a 14-year-old and had a passion for other sports such as cricket, golf, and rugby. Ernie needed to make some choices, especially if he wanted to be a competitive player. As he grew older and his physique became bigger, he chose golf, which he began playing at the age of nine with his grandfather. "I was becoming too slow and cumbersome for competitive tennis." It is true that Els, a South African, hardly has the figure of a keen sportsman. At 6' 4", he is built like a boxer, which has given him a rhythmic and generous swing. He plays with a calm but powerful force. Players on the Tour tend to acquire nicknames, and Ernie is no exception. His size and shape have inspired comparison with Fred Couples, with whom he shares the name, the Big Easy.

A Huge Talent

In the early 1990s, Norman, Faldo, Price, Couples, and Stewart—the old guard, all of whom were over 35—were masters of the Tours and monopolized the prize money. Ernie's imposing figure stood out among these stars from 1992 onward. He finished fifth in the British Open on the hideously difficult Muirfield course, dominated only

(Preceding page) *His relaxed attitude serves him well in his aim for big targets—the Majors.*

by Nick Faldo. It was a good year for Els, who won six competitions on the African Tour, three of them in South Africa, a feat which only Gary Player had achieved before him. In 1993, Ernie proved that he was aiming at the Majors. At the Royal St. George's, the year of Norman's second victory, he finished sixth in the British Open, breaking 70 in all four rounds—the only player to achieve that feat. One month earlier, he was classed seventh in the U.S. Open behind the astonishing Lee Janzen. Composure and freedom seem to be his two favorite words. Els does a lot of traveling and plays in various Tours; he won the only victory that same year in Japan.

Els Doesn't Put All His Eggs in One Basket

When a South African player reaches a level at which he can compete abroad, he begins by playing in the European Tour. Ernie followed this route, as had Player and Price before him. Unlike Norman, he is not determined to win a maximum number of tournaments at all cost. Els is not a giant, but rather a gourmet, and the taste of a Major means more to him than amassing victories in the other tournaments. In his six years on the Tours, Ernie ranked 60th in the United States, having won just over $3 million, and twelfth in Europe, having won $4,400,000. If these amounts are significant, they are still far less than the prize money awarded to Norman or Elkington. But at the age of 27, Els can boast a splendid record in the Majors—one which any champion would envy.

WITH NELSON MANDELA

A supporter to reckon with.

"Nobody ever swung the club too slowly."

Bobby Jones

AN ATHLETIC STATURE

U.S. PGA 1995, Riviera Country Club, Los Angeles.

THE RECIPE FOR HIS SWING

Fullness, rhythm, controlled power.

U.S. OPEN 1994, OAKMONT

Inimitable on the greens as usual.

His First Major, the U.S. Open

In 1994, Ernie was well-placed to win his first Major. His opponent, Colin Montgomerie, was a player of similar skill who wanted as much as he did to win a Grand Slam event. The Scotsman had had a foretaste of victory in the U.S. Open in the year in which Kite achieved the crowning moment of his career at Pebble Beach. Ernie and Colin were on a par, but Els, the younger man, sent his older rival packing in the playoff. That year, Colin seemed to be suffering from fatigue and the heat. Oakmont was another setback for the Scotsman though it was far from his last disappointment. Els continued the season by coming eighth in the U.S. PGA. He also joined the European Tour and achieved some good results, winning the World Match Play Championship and playing well in the Dubai Desert Classic and the Johnnie Walker Championship. The following year was one of transition with few wins and only one Top Ten in the Majors. For the second year running, Els won World Match Play Championship.

Relaxation is an integral part of Els's personality.

Two Seasons Without a Major

Ernie needs to learn to manage his time so that he gets long breaks. In 1995, he won the Byron Nelson Classic, and in 1996 the Buick Classic. His periods off the greens allowed him to be fresher than the competition by the end of the season. In 1996 he won the World Match Play Championship for the third time and the World Cup for the first time. Ernie has found out what works best for him and knows how best to plan his year. He lives in Orlando, Florida, where he can indulge his love of water sports, though he is still looking for the right place to build his dream home. Quality of life means more to him than prizes: "I know I can still win the Majors. I have the strength and the will power. The fact that Tiger Woods is on my trail doesn't scare me. I wouldn't like to live like him. At 21, he's so famous that he can't move around without a bodyguard. Life can't be easy for him. I wouldn't swap our destinies for all the gold in the world, although I enjoy playing against him."

141

ERNIE ELS

BORN OCTOBER 17, 1969
IN JOHANNESBURG, RSA

ENGAGED TO BE MARRIED

2 MAJORS
U.S. OPEN 1994–97

25 PRO WINS

LIVES IN ORLANDO, FLORIDA
AND FANCOURT, RSA

U.S. OPEN 1997, CONGRESSIONAL

Letting off steam, having beaten Montgomerie and Lehman.

A Magnificent Second Major

Els vacations for at least six weeks in winter so that he can ease back into form by late March. "Mickelson got back into shape very quickly this year, as he usually does. He's a player I like competing against on the Tour, not because I defeated him in the World Junior in San Diego, but because I really believe that his abilities have been underestimated. When Woods dominated the Masters, I was not yet at my best. I felt I was getting into my best form in Europe, during the PGA Championship at Wentworth in May." Everything there depended on how the final holes were played by Jeff Maggert, Tom Lehman, Colin Montgomerie, and Ernie Els. Woods was out of contention. Maggert was the first to get in trouble. At the 17th hole of the Congressional, Lehman's ball landed in the water. Els, who was farther away from the flag, had to play before Colin. The Big Easy produced a five-iron shot that dropped within six feet of the cup. This was a crushing blow to the Scotsman. He almost sent a six-iron into the water. The calm strength of the South African inflicted another blow to Montgomerie.

Ernie Els is the only player under 30 to have two Majors under his belt. Until the age of 14, he dreamed of winning the Men's Singles at Wimbledon; he doesn't mind too much that he opted for golf instead. Ever since his second victory in the U.S. Open, the Big Easy is a clear favorite in all the Majors because he is good at all aspects of the game. His formula is to concentrate on the Majors, break up his season with long gaps, and take care in every shot he takes.

WITH HIS FAMILY

With his parents and the U.S. Open trophy.

colin montgomerie

FAVORITE TO WIN THE BRITISH OPEN 1997

With his father who was then secretary of the Royal Troon Golf Club.

The best European golfer of our time is also one of the strongest personalities of the Tour. In 1997, Colin Montgomerie came first in the Order of Merit for the fifth year running! This remarkable performance demonstrates the consistency and maturity of this 34-year-old player. Yet he is now faced with a dilemma: should he continue to play on the European tour or move to the United States to further his career goals and aspiration? Despite eleven profitable years, in which he has become the biggest prizewinner on the European circuit, the Scotsman has by no means exhausted his ambitions.

Pride and Ambition

Colin is not only the leading British golfer, he also has a degree in management from the University of Houston. The time spent in Texas has opened his eyes to the wide world and he has proven he can hold his own in international competition. His victories in the Scottish Strokeplay and the Scottish Amateur have also allowed him to become a member of many national and international teams. The only major setback for Montgomerie was when José-Maria Olazábal dealt him his first crushing defeat in 1984.

SEARCH FOR THE HOLY GRAIL

(Preceding page) *In the eyes of the public, Colin's grimaces too often spoil his performance.*

THE RYDER CUP

Monty has become a European team stalwart.

Montgomerie recovered emotionally and set off to conquer new territory, confident that his unorthodox style and impressive credentials were hard to beat. Colin has an eye on the international scene and his ambitions have led him beyond the frontiers of Great Britain. In 1987, he turned professional on the strength of his plus-three handicap. He had great ambitions of becoming a top player, winning the Claret Jug and wearing the Green Jacket.

A Seasoned Character

Colin used to take himself far too seriously, and soon began to show Faldo-like bouts of ill temper. His imperious shouts of, "Stand still, please," did not find favor with the gallery. Even today he is not a favorite with the public or the press, whom he often snubs. After 1987, his successes dwindled to a trickle. In 1987, Colin's father became secretary of the Troon Golf Club and this brought him back to his hometown.

Colin did not finish among the top five until 1991 when he won the Scandinavian Open. The following year, the Scotsman's game improved considerably and his

ST. ANDREWS, 1995

(Following pages) *His unique style translates itself in the suppleness of his finish.*

COLIN MONTGOMERIE

BORN JUNE 23, 1963
IN GLASGOW, SCOTLAND

MARRIED, 2 CHILDREN

MAJOR: not yet

16 PRO WINS

RYDER CUP
1991-93-95-97

LIVES IN OXSHOTT, SURREY,
ENGLAND

ALFRED DUNHILL CUP

	TEAM						TEAM				
	ZIMBABWE						INDIA				
	SCOTLAND						SWEDEN				
	SOUTH AFRICA						CANADA				
	IRELAND						WALES				
	NEW ZEALAND						GERMANY				
	AUSTRALIA						JAPAN				
	UNITED STATES						ITALY				
	SPAIN						ENGLAND				

Callaway GOLF Big Bertha

Big Bertha

COLIN MONTGOMERIE

BIG BERTHA

ALFRED DUNHILL CUP

average score was among some of the best. In 1992, he finished amaong the top five in a the U.S. Open. On the last day he started off far from the leaders, but was in first place when he finished, though a lot of players still had to complete their rounds. Montgomerie stayed in the top rankings, however, and only Jeff Sultan and Tom Kite, the winner, did better.

Missed Opportunities

The Ryder Cup (three wins, including one against Janzen in a singles match) and two European titles, including the Volvo Masters, put him at the top of the Order of Merit for 1993. Yet in June, he was badly beaten by Ernie Els in the U.S. Open. At Oakmont, he saw the young South African beat him in the playoff. His third defeat came in the 1995 U.S. PGA where he was surpassed by Australian Steve Elkington. Colin returned to Europe bitterly disappointed. Nevertheless, he managed to win the German Masters and the Lancôme Trophy, coming top in the European rankings for the third time in a row.

CHANGES OF MOOD

A basic need to express himself.

"An excellent golfer and a great thinker, but a bit of a prima donna, and always looking for perfection."

RYDER CUP 1997, VALDERRAMA

On September 28, playing against Scott Hoch, he won the half-point which led to victory.

A More Fulfilling 1996

As some of the leading players on the European Tour lost their momentum, Colin's career took off again. "Monty," as he was nicknamed, was 33 years old in 1996 and his playoff defeats began to worry him, though he attributed them to fatigue. He decided to lose weight, and emerged a new man at the beginning of the season—a dangerous opponent for his competitors. Monty won three victories and a fourth top ranking in the Order of Merit on the European Tour, though the news was not so good in the Grand Slam. At the end of the year, however, he won an important playoff against the man who had deprived him of the U.S. Open two years earlier—Ernie Els. "It was the first time my father had ever watched me winning and I was delighted that it was in a playoff. I was able to prove that I could play under pressure and sink important putts." There must be a lot of history in the relationship between James Montgomerie and Colin for the son to react in this way. This father-and-son conflict is comparable to Norman's relationship with his parents. Each man wanted to prove to his father that he could follow his own path to success: in Colin's case, his father brought him up in a strict Scottish tradition which doesn't favor the individuality that top-level golf seems to require.

A New Man

Monty has gained maturity and is able to view events more objectively as he grows older and his play improves. He has become one of the sages of the European tour, and takes it upon himself to speak out whenever he finds anything wrong with its organization. His early arrogance has been transformed into a real sense of responsibility. Ballesteros said in 1997 that the Scotsman had become the key player on his team and that he was counting on his experience and common sense. Yet this doesn't mean that Monty wasn't fazed again by his old rival, Ernie Els, in the Congressional at Bethesda in 1997. Once again, a single shot was all that stood between Colin and victory at the U.S. Open. This is a tournament that suits him to a tee, with his dead-straight drive and brilliant putting. And yet Els dealt him such a blow at the 17th that Monty found it hard to recover. With a five-iron, Els's first stroke put him only four feet from the hole. There was nothing Montgomerie could do.

On the European side of the pond, Monty won two events in 1997 and was coming close to becoming the first golfer to finish first five times in a row in the Order of Merit, one more than Peter Oosterhuis. Montgomerie's career peaked in September 1997 with his performance in the Ryder Cup. It was he who scored the half-point that enabled Europe to win the confrontation, 14–13. He finally beat his old rival Ernie Els as well as Davis Love in 1998 in the finals of the Andersen Consulting World Championship, also known as the World Match Play Championship.

A ROUND WITH CINDY CRAWFORD

Montgomerie is full of good advice....

DAVIS LOVE III

SKILLED USE OF THE SAND WEDGE

You don't become a force to be reckoned with on the Tour unless your short game is good.

In the Love family, there is a line of succession not only in name but in a shared love of golf. Davis Love, Jr., son of the original Davis Love, was a golf pro himself by the time his eldest son was born. Davis Love III thus came into contact with the best American golfers of the day. The Tour became his back yard. Young Davis was a good golfer, playing on the university team at the University of North Carolina and turning pro in 1985. His daughter, Alexia, was born in 1988, the year in which her grandfather was killed in a fatal air crash. His death meant the loss of one of the greatest pro teachers on the Tour.

From Davis Love, Jr. to Davis Love III

Davis Love, Jr., had become something of a guru in the golf teaching world. In 1986 David Love III became a pro, but for three years, his highest position in the

DAVIS AND MARK LOVE III AT THE 1997 U.S. PGA

(Preceding page) *The Love family had hoped for this victory for three generations.*

IN THE 1997 RYDER CUP

Valderrama was not his best memory of the season.

A GREAT MATCH

Love's victory over Rocca at the Belfry in the 1993 Ryder Cup saved the Cup for the United States.

rankings was 33rd. In fact, prior to 1988, he only made the cut once out of seven Grand Slam events.

The Early Years

Davis lost his father and mentor in 1988, at a time when he badly needed to improve his scores, but in the following two seasons his game improved spectacularly, earning him wins in the International and the great Heritage Classic, played on the very narrow Hilton Head, South Carolina course. The 1991 season put Love in the Top Ten in the rankings. Winning the Players Championship, the Heritage Classic, and the Greater Greensboro Open, Davis found himself runner up in the Order of Merit, and was selected to play in both the Dunhill Cup and the World Cup.

WELL-LIKED BY THE GREAT PLAYERS

His "Mr. Nice Guy" image is acknowledged by Couples and Norman.

Still Waiting to Win a Major

To win a Major, match play skills are needed. A player needs to know when to go on the offensive and how to sink high-pressure putts. Although Davis Love III's basic game is equal to that of a Watson or a Nicklaus, he lacks aggression, especially in his putting, at crucial moments. Davis has had two particularly painful experiences in this regard. The first was during the Masters in 1995, when he started off the last round with a score of 66, but ended up one shot behind Ben Crenshaw. When he took fourth place in the U.S. Open that same year, he ended the year having broken the million-dollar mark in prize money. With his golfing heritage, Davis, whose father nearly won the Masters in 1964, knows just how important the Majors are to his career. Finishing second the following year was a cruel blow. He should never have let victory elude him on the last green at Oakland Hills. Of course, he was under extreme pressure from his opponents and three-putted the final hole. Mistakes made by unreliable putters like Lehman and Love gave Steve Jones, whose putting is near-perfect, a chance for victory that would otherwise have been completely beyond his reach.

Relief at the U.S. Open

Davis felt that this U.S. Open, played at the Winged Foot course, might give him the chance to overcome his reputation of being "the best player never to have won a Major." The Loves do everything as a family, and his brother, Mark, is also his caddie. Davis Love, Jr.'s two sons were full of confidence in the practice matches at Mamaroneck,

GOLF: A FAMILY TRADITION

(Following pages) *Davis Love, Jr. would have been very proud of his two sons.*

BIRDIE AT 18TH AT WINGED FOOT

The 1997 U.S. PGA and the joy of finally winning a Major.

scoring 66-71-66 after three rounds. Only one of Love's opponents, though a formidable one, was at 7 under, which equaled the two brothers' score. The culprit was Justin Leonard, who set the course record with a 65. At the age of 33, in his twelfth season on the Tour and nine years after his father's death, Davis would produce the best drives and approach shots of his life. He remained undeterred by Leonard's challenge. Surprises, however, were still in store. It had been raining since daybreak, but the rain suddenly stopped and the clouds parted. A magnificent rainbow appeared over the last green when the two brothers were making for the 18th hole. "Did you see that rainbow, he's there with us, he's watching us," Davis confided in his brother Mark. There was a flood of emotion as the Love clan rushed over to embrace the winner, Davis Love III, with little Davis Love IV on the green, and Davis Love, Jr., looking down on his son's moment of triumph.

A Ryder Cup Player Since 1993

Love and Kite are the most experienced and successful Ryder Cup players. They won their first doubles match at the Belfry in 1993. It was a handsome victory, snatched from the likes of Ballesteros and Olazábal. But the Spanish pair took revenge in the next two matches. In the singles, Davis Love III defeated Costantino Rocca, who appeared to

THE 1997 U.S. PGA: HUGS AND RELIEF

A hug for his mother, an accolade for Justin Leonard.

panic when faced with the possibility of victory. This manifested itself at the 17th hole when Rocca was overcome with fear and missed a three-foot putt. Love III caught up with him and crucified him on the 18th green. The defeat of the Italian gave Davis the winning point to tip the balance and enabled the United States to beat Europe 15-13. In the 1995 Ryder Cup, during the Rochester match on the Oak Hill course, Costantino succumbed to another avalanche of winning shots and bowed before his opponent. Rocca would recover a few years later at Valderrama, where he withstood the pressure and managed to beat Tiger Woods. When Davis made his third appearance in the Ryder Cup he had a Major to his credit. Unfortunately, the title did not bring him luck—he did not win a single point in the four singles matches he played.

A Product of the U.S. Tour

Nevertheless, 1997 was a great year for Davis, with four wins and third place in the Order of Merit. His prize money amounted to $1,635,953—making him the sixth-richest golfer in the world with a total of $8,470,982. Davis Love is the classic product of the American Tour, clean-cut, polite, well-dressed, conservative, and competitive. Now that he has several winning years behind him, Davis may find his love of golfing architecture becomes a vehicle for self-expression in the future.

José-Maria

OLAZABAL

Xhema (pronounced Jama, to rhyme with pa-jama) is the Spanish nickname of José-Maria Olazábal, just as Seve is Ballesteros's nickname. Olazábal, a Basque, was in the forefront of the new talent in the 1980s.

Little José Was Almost Born on the Golf Course
Olazábal's parents worked at the Royal San Sebastian Golf Course and his parents used to take him to the golf club as a child. José would spend the day playing golf. At the age of seven, he won the Junior Championship of Spain for the under-tens. At the age of thirteen he was already a scratch player (with a 0 handicap). From then on, his rise was meteoric. Xhema was completely self-taught and yet he had acquired a classic swing. He even beat consistently good players, such as Colin Montgomerie, who lost to Olazábal five and four in the final of the British Amateur at Formby in 1984.

An Unbeatable Amateur Record Before Turning Pro
In 1983, Olazábal carried off both the Italian and the Spanish Amateur Opens, followed next year by the Belgian Junior International. Xhema won the Boy's Amateur (1983), the Youth Championship (1985), and finally the British Amateur (1984), which earned him an invitation to play in the Masters for the first time in 1985. The young Basque eventually took the decision to turn pro and passed the heats to get his card. For Olazábal, this prolonged and demanding series of matches was a pushover, and he easily won first place, beating six hundred other competitors. In his first year on the Tour he achieved victories in the Sanyo and the Swiss Open. In 1987, his career quietened down, but he was back in form once again in Belgium, winning the Volvo Open. He also carried off the German Masters. In the next three years, he was among the top three in the European Order of Merit, with victories in Tenerife and in the Dutch Open, as well as an initial victory in the Japanese Tour in the Visa Masters.

Welcome to the United States
Olazábal had little left to prove in Europe and left for the United States to seek victory at one of the three Majors played on American soil. This gifted young man was

WEARING NAVY BLUE LIKE BALLESTEROS?

Xhema does not look at all like Seve, his hero.

FAME AND SUFFERING

(Previous page) *Golf has been the whole life of this mountain boy born on the golf course.*

167

U.S. MASTERS 1994

An occasion for a demonstration of emotion.

eagerly awaited, so that he could demonstrate his talents in the Grand Slam events.
Success came first of all in the Golf World Series, which Olazábal breezed through,
winning by twelve shots over his nearest rival, Lanny Wadkins. In Europe, he won
three more victories, the Benson and Hedges, Carrols Irish, and the Lancôme Trophy.
Xhema now had four victories in Europe and one in the United States (The International in 1991) but fared less well in 1993. He lost the consistency of his drive and
suddenly, his confidence went as well. It was at this point he consulted John Jacobs,
the famous English pro and father of the European Tour who helped him radically
alter his swing.

An Extraordinary Ryder Cup Player
Olazábal rejoined the European team at Muirfield in 1987 and partnered with
Ballesteros. These two players complemented each other and were close as brothers, being largely responsible for the first ever European Ryder Cup win on American soil by 15 to 13 at Muirfield Village, Ohio. José-Maria continued to do
brilliantly in 1989, bringing his number of match victories to eight in a period of
just two years.

VICTORIOUS

Winning the U.S. Masters in 1994.

The Spanish Enigma and the Masters

In early 1994, Olazábal traveled to Augusta. His short game was brilliant, he putted and hit approach shots better than anyone. Only Tom Lehman, who was in the lead after three rounds, managed to catch up with him, but it was in vain. Once again, a Spaniard would wear the Green Jacket. There was everything to play for at the 15th, where the Spaniard sank an eagle putt. Lehman's game collapsed and Xhema won the match by two shots. Yet as he donned the Green Jacket, the young Basque was unaware that he would soon experience some of the worst moments of his life.

A Forced Two Year Withdrawal

Shortly thereafter, Olazábal began to experience agonizing pains in his feet, which seriously affected the start of his 1995 season. He managed to win one doubles match, the Perrier Tournament in Paris, partnered by the ever-faithful Severiano Ballesteros. But José could bear it no longer, his toes were hurting too much. Although he was operated on for rheumatoid arthritis the pain continued. Xhema stayed at home in Fuenterabbia, consoled by his parents. He had to forego the 1995 Ryder Cup and became totally demoralized. The whole of 1996 was spent between operations and recuperation, but nothing

AUGUSTA 1991, A BUNKER AT THE 18TH

(Following pages) *Even then, Olazábal was close to winning the Green Jacket.*

JOSÉ-MARIA OLAZÁBAL

BORN ON FEBRUARY 5, 1966
AT FUENTERRABIA, SPAIN

UNMARRIED

1 MAJOR
MASTERS 1994

23 PRO WINS

RYDER CUP
1987-89-91-93-97

LIVES AT FUENTERRABIA, SP.

A BROTHERLY UNDERSTANDING WITH BALLESTEROS

The two Spaniards confer during the 1997 Ryder Cup.

helped. There was even a time when Xhema could not even walk, even crutches weren't enough; he was confined to a wheelchair. Medical science was confounded by his case, since he would not respond to treatment. However, a glimmer of hope appeared when he was told that a German practitioner of alternative medicine, Dr. Hans Wilhelm Muller-Wohlfart, might be able to help him.

Return of the Prodigal Son

The German doctor had diagnosed a hernia of the disks between the fifth lumbar and the first sacral vertebrae. José-Maria slowly began to recover but was unable to take part in the first five tournaments because his feet were still not able to carry him through four rounds of competition. In late February, he chose Dubai for his first appearance. "Ollie," as the British call him, had just celebrated his 31st birthday and was thrilled to discover that his game was gradually returning to form. In his third tournament, the Canaries Open, he hit a hole in one and won the event, beating the rising English star, Lee Westwood, with scores of 70-67-68-67. At the last putt, the Basque was moved to tears. "You know, I don't show my feelings easily, but this is an unbelievable moment. A few months ago, I thought I would never be able to play golf again, nor even walk. You cannot imagine my happiness at finally being able to accept the invitation to the Masters knowing that I am back to my old standard."

Ballesteros, the Ryder Cup, and Emotion

José-Maria Olazábal was much missed on the European golfing scene during those painful 18 months of forced withdrawal. His unexpected return to the 1997 Ryder Cup team was a great moment for his friend and team captain Severiano. Seve's daring move in pairing his young compatriot with Costantino Rocca paid off, since they won two of the three doubles they played together. Partnered with Ignacio Garrido, Xhema played very well against Mickelson and Lehman. On the evening of the European victory, Ballesteros ended the press conference by asking each member of his team to say a few words. José was the first. "This victory fills me with joy, I don't have to remind you that only a few months ago I was considered to be finished with golf." Xhema was unable to continue, he was so overcome with emotion. Rocca was then seen to take his friend's hand, and put an arm around his shoulders, both himself and Seve weeping tears of emotion.

AN UNEXPECTED RETURN TO THE COURSES

Olazábal thought his career was over but he became a winner again in March 1997 at Las Palomas.

Phil Mickelson

"Isn't it logical for right-handed players to play like left-handers? Bob Charles is right-handed as well."

There isn't a golfer alive with more talent for the short game than magic Mickelson. He's at his best with a sand wedge in his hand. Sand-trap shots, lobbed shots, backspin—he's a master of all the techniques. This San Diegan is one of the few left-handed Tour players and certainly the best since New Zealander Bob Charles won the British Open in 1963.

A Remarkable Amateur Career

Mickelson has won the Walker Cup twice, the NCAA championships (1989, 1990, and 1992) three times, and one U.S. Amateur (1990), a record topped only recently by the whirlwind Tiger Woods. Phil has been crazy about sports since childhood, a passion that runs in the family. Mickelson senior is a pilot and former ski champion who took his son out with him to play golf when the toddler was only 18 months old. Later, he tried to teach him to play right-handed, but Mickelson junior preferred to be a southpaw. His well-built, 6' 2" frame helps him drive very long shots, and in combination with a great short game he is a formidable match. Mickelson is a worthy contender, along with Ben Crenshaw, for

THE ONLY LEFT-HANDER AMONG THE ELITE

On the golf course he does everything differently.

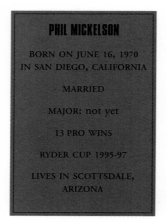

PHIL MICKELSON

BORN ON JUNE 16, 1970
IN SAN DIEGO, CALIFORNIA

MARRIED

MAJOR: not yet

13 PRO WINS

RYDER CUP 1995-97

LIVES IN SCOTTSDALE,
ARIZONA

the title of the best putter in the world. In fact, the two men are close friends. Mickelson has made a close study of the great players and retains a precise mental image of each of their swings without ever having known them. When playing a round, he may think of Bob Jones when he needs to get a rhythm to his swings or of Ben Hogan when the ball needs to make a penetrating trajectory.

He Wants to Win More Tournaments Before Turning Pro

As an amateur champion, Mickelson has been invited to play at various Opens. He took advantage of the invitation to play in the Northern Telecom Open to take a professional trophy right out from under the noses of such pros as Bob Tway and Tom Purtzer. His caddie, Steve Loy, was his coach at college and later accompanied him to Cornerstone, his management agency (a rival to IMG). This victory repeated that of Texan amateur Scott Verplank six years earlier.

ELEGANT AND POWERFUL

Teeing off at Augusta in 1995.

Nothing and no one could stop Phil from turning pro in June 1992. He played in ten competitions, performing well enough to win his Tournament card. Only a year later, he had his first win, on home territory at the Buick Invitational at Torrey Pines Golf Club. That year, his achievements won him a place among the first 25 plays in the Order of Merit. In 1994, he did even better, gaining a place in the Millionaires' Club thanks to his victory in the Mercedes Championship.

1995: An Unspectacular Year With the Exception of the Ryder Cup
Phil was chasing the Major that the press kept assuring him was "in the bag" after he came in third in the U.S. PGA. While on the Tour, he gained an important victory at the Northern Telecom Open—this time as a professional—but dropped back slightly in the Order of Merit, down to 28th, although he attained his second million in prize money. This was also the first time he was picked for the Ryder Cup team. His talents in match

play were a sensation. He won all three of the matches with great aplomb. Per Ulrik Johansson played a singles and a foursome match against Mickelson and lost each time. Whether partnered with Corey Pavin or Jay Haas, Phil was unbeatable.

The Romantic Ending to 1996
Phil's year began very well, with wins in two of the first three tournaments in his calendar. Mickelson seems to do best in hot weather and close to home either in Arizona or California. Having won the Nortel and the Phoenix Open, he won the Order of Merit ranking for the first time. Despite these two new trophies, he soon had to concede to a man who was having a strong year: Tom Lehman, winner of the British Open, beat him in the Tour Championship played at the Southern Hills Country Club in Tulsa, Oklahoma, before the tournament was moved to the Champions Golf Club in Houston, in 1997. Phil's two other wins enabled him to end the year with a personal best in prize money—$1,697,799 in a single year! The Byron Nelson Classic and the World Series of Golf were two more successes to crown his marriage to Amy McBride in late November, 1996.

But Where Are the Majors?
Phil did well in 1996, coming in third in the Masters and eighth in the U.S. PGA, although he had yet to win a single event in the Grand Slam. The next year, he did not even make it to the top 20, and in Augusta he didn't make the cut. He is best at the long game and the Augusta fairways are wide. The worst thing that can happen to a player is to be labeled "Best player never to have won a Major." It's happened to Mickelson, who is in the company of the unlucky Montgomerie, at least at the end of the 1997 season. Of course, he has plenty of time left. He's only 27 years old and Kite was 42 before he won his first Major title.

1997: A Year of Transition
Mickelson achieved the 11th win of his career at Castle Rock, Colorado, in early August. This tournament is played as a Stableford and favors those players with an aggressive temperament, a format which perfectly suited Mickelson. To give an idea of the kind of game he played in the Sprint International, his choice of clubs at the 14th

WITH A SAND WEDGE IN HIS HANDS, HE CAN DO ANYTHING

His father had built him a green and a sand-trap in his back yard.

hole, a par five 623-yards long, is indicative. Phil was on cloud nine. Playing under normal conditions, he used a driver, followed by a six-iron to get to the green. These were two huge shots! According to the official statistics of the U.S. Tour, Phil's 284-yard average places him fifth in length of drives. The Castle Rock win also assured him a place on the Ryder Cup team for the second time. Mickelson won his singles match against Darren Clarke; he drew in two doubles and was defeated in the BBB four-some in which he partnered Davis Love III. The two drawn matches were in part-nership with Tom Lehman, his favorite golfing partner. Yet twice, the young Ignacio Garrido, paired first with Jesper Parnevik, then with José-Maria Olazábal, was to square the American duo. Tom sunk a two-yard putt on the gentle slope of the 18th green to draw one of the two matches in which he admitted never having been under such pressure before.

A Bright Future

Thanks to his two 1997 wins, Phil is now eleventh in the Order of Merit and has won $5 million in prize money over his six years on the Tour, putting him in 37th place overall. By the end of 1997, he had won the most money of any player in the first six years of his career. Many have tried to get a clear idea of the personality of this rather reserved man. The press never manages to faze him, though he did have a few run-ins with them in Ireland, when he made a rash comment during a Walker Cup meet. This experience has made him more cautious. However, he is also a master at the devastating remark, whether ironic or darkly humorous, and he is a mischievous joker. The dry atmosphere of the American Tour is still rather traditional and conservative, with more emphasis on religion than fun, as is clearly evidenced by the winners' speeches. He reserves his puns and opinions for his nearest and dearest —a pity for the public. In addition, his study at the University of Arizona has also been valuable on the Tour. Mickelson understands how American society works, and the next time he decides to show his feelings, it will be on the 18th green, after sinking the winning putt in a Major!

This could well happen in 1998, for he had a brilliant start in winning the first tournament of the season, the Mercedes Championship played on the La Costa course at Carlsbad, California. Mickelson is used to victories early in the season on the West Coast. This may well be a sign that he needs less preparation than do some other players, and plays best after quite a long break. The key to the Majors for him may well lie—as it does for Els and Couples—in taking a vacation before the big meets.

WITH HIS WIFE, AMY

His most faithful supporter.

THE 1995 U.S. OPEN, SHINNECOCK HILLS

The best player in the world never to have won a Major may well end up winning one…

JUSTIN
LEONARD

JUSTIN LEONARD

BORN JUNE 15, 1972
IN DALLAS, TEXAS

UNMARRIED

1 MAJOR
BRITISH OPEN 1997

3 PRO WINS

RYDER CUP 1997

LIVES IN DALLAS, TEXAS

DAVID DUVAL'S AMERICAN DREAM

David Duval's case is quite different from that of Justin Leonard. The son of professional golfer Bob Duval took the classic route, passing through all the conventional stages, from junior and university teams to the Satellite Tour. David turned professional at the age of 22 and won two victories on the Nike Tour, before joining the Major Tour in 1993. Duval may not be as spectacularly talented as Mickelson, Leonard, or Woods but he is nevertheless a force to be reckoned with. His great asset is his exceptional knack for producing birdies. After 92 tournaments on the American Tour, in which he came second seven times, his luck finally changed and he won the Michelob Championship in October 1997. It was a turning point for Duval; at the age of 26, he produced three wins in a row, including the famous and well-endowed Tour Championship.

Duval has a sturdy build; he works hard at his game and is a solid and reliable player. Like Paul Stankowsky or Stewart Cink, he is one of the new wave of golfers. Duval's success shows that the traditional route for American golfers produces great players. Duval, a native of Jacksonville, Florida, came second in the 1997 Order of Merit, right behind Tiger Woods, by amassing some $1,885,308 in prize money (a total of more than four million dollars for the first five years of his career as a professional golfer).

A UNIQUE STYLE
*Some people compare Leonard's clumsy swing
to the movement of a baseball pitcher!*

WITH TIGER WOODS

Two opposing styles but a single ambition—to be the best.

It's as if there were a Texan golf fairy. Once upon a time, in the 1920s, this fairy met two young men at the Glen Garden Country Club. Both were the same age; one was called Ben and the other Byron. After she had introduced herself, the boys shyly asked the fairy to make them into golf champions like Bob Jones or Walter Hagen. The fairy had fallen under the spell of this sport and granted their wish. Thirty years later, she realized that her protégés were older and went in search of new ones. With a wave of her magic wand, she bestowed the gift of golf upon little Tom Kite. In order to be sure that at least one Texan was at the top of the profession, she bewitched young Ben Crenshaw, who was only eight years old at the time. Delighted with the results achieved by her protégés, but noticing that the sport had changed in some respects, the fairy decided to adjust her spell, adding to it length of drive. "And you will have an easier wrist release, so that you can hit the ball more than 300 yards," she told Frederick Couples. The good Texan fairy then discovered Justin Leonard. "He must have a lot of cool, this little Justin, so I'll ensure he makes his mark on the Tour quite quickly."

A Long Career Started Early

The ways to the top are well-defined in the United States. Justin Leonard chose the classic route, and tried his luck on the University of Texas team. The years he spent

THE UNEXPECTED AT TROON IN 1997

(*Preceding pages*) *At the eighteenth hole, he hugged the Claret Jug.*

"More organized than the Pentagon, Justin is a redoubtable predator."

with the best university players and the best amateurs in the country would give him experience and a taste for victory. He made an impressive start, winning the Southwest Conference Championship four times in a row, the U.S. Amateur in 1992, and walked away with the NCAA Championship in 1994. Justin represented his country in the Amateur World Championships in 1992 and in the 1993 Walker Cup. Upon graduation in 1994, he turned professional. The decision was made with little hesitation because, as an amateur, he had already had a taste of the Tour on seven occasions and had succeeded in five cuts, finishing among the top 25, an indication of his burgeoning talent.

First Seasons on the Tour

The first season was a way of making contact. His 126th ranking in the Order of Merit enabled Leonard to avoid having to compete in the heats. That year, he only played in 13 tournaments, finishing among the top ten in two and coming in third in one of them. In the following season in 1995, his performance was undistinguished, although he came in eighth in the U.S. PGA and seventh on the Tour Championship. These two achievements had an enormous effect on his confidence, however. Justin began to believe firmly in his abilities. "My place is on the podium—I can get there," he claimed to his close friends. It was not until his third year, in 1996, that Leonard achieved his first win, at the Buick Open. He scored 65-64-69-68 on the Warwick Hills course. He finished five up on his nearest rival, Chip Beck, and won a check for $216,000, the biggest win of his career. The Tour had witnessed the birth of a predator.

The Spiritual Heir to Hogan, Kite, and Crenshaw

As a teenager, Justin grew up in the shadow of his heroes. He was inspired by Crenshaw's putting and Kite's short game. Leonard has never been an imitator, but gains inspiration from others. The books written by Penick and Hogan hold proud places on Justin's bookshelves. The basics of his swing were taught him by the pro at his club, the Royal Oaks Country Club in Dallas. Randy Smith had been following Justin's development from the first time he discovered golf. The special features of his swing made Leonard play a very straight ball right down the middle of the fairway.

HIS EYES ARE A NATURAL WEAPON

(Previous page) *He is also good at analyzing distances and angles just like his Texan predecessor, Ben Hogan.*

BRITISH OPEN 1997: A SPECTACULAR VICTORY

A round of 65 on his card.

As Trevino says of him: "He's so straight he could play in a canyon." But his straight game is not Leonard's deadliest weapon. Justin's swing may not be the most academic on the Tour—quite the opposite. But in golf, "It's not how but how many," that counts. He is certainly skilled and has hints of Hogan's style, which is based on a movement that keeps the ball in play. Leonard's coolness and determination ensure that he will be around for a long time.

Texas Before the West Coast of Scotland

In Scotland, Ben Hogan was nicknamed the "Wee Ice-Mon." The imperturbable winner of the British Open in 1953 at Carnoustie was not what might be described as a sympathetic and charismatic player. He was indeed worthy of the epithet "little ice man." Leonard has the same attitude on the course, imperturbable and determined. Unlike Ben Hogan, however, Justin is much more sympathetic and forthcoming outside the game. The two men did not have the same upbringing. Leonard's determination enabled him to win the Kemper Open in early June, just before the second Major of the year. It was an unexpected victory. A catastrophic 78 in the third round of the U.S. Open prevented Leonard from doing well in the famous Congressional Course at Bethesda, Maryland. Els, Montgomerie, Lehman, and Maggert were able to fight it out between them without having to fear Leonard at their heels. At the next Grand Slam meeting, the British Open, Leonard left for Troon, having decided to prepare conscientiously for this tournament because he would need to make it through preliminary rounds. He played the course at least five times before the first round, leaving nothing to chance. Justin is just as hard-working as he is particular. At home, he is scrupulously tidy, and everything has a place. Everything he undertakes must be carefully structured, like his overall strategy and his scrupulously planned putting.

At Troon for the British Open, He Believed He'd Win from the First

Leonard was determined to make sure he had all the cards in his favor. He was by no means the favorite for this Major, although he had four top tens under his belt, won in the previous years of the Tour Championship and the U.S. PGA. His first two scores, 69-66, positioned him comfortably. In a first windy tour, he went around in thirty-five shots without touching a green! He played approach shots followed by a

A devastating putter.

single putt. His putting was devastating. Lehman and Pavin are known for the precision of their long putts, just as Els and Mickelson are famous for their putts of less than 10 feet. But Justin is dangerous anywhere on a green. The third round did not live up to his expectations because he finished with a score of 72. He did much better, however, in the fourth round. This future winner spent a long Saturday evening session on the putting green to restore his confidence. The next morning, his caddie, Bob Riefke, remembers: "He simply hit eight balls with his one-iron. His eyes were open wider than usual and I knew it was going to be a great day." Six birdies over the first nine holes, and two pars saved for the notoriously difficult 11th and 15th holes, two very long par fours, followed by two unforgettable birdies at the 16th (par five) and 17th (par three) earned him a 65 and a victory.

EIGHT BIRDIES IN THE LAST TOUR AT TROON!

He triumphed at the 2nd, 3rd, 4th, 6th, 7th, 9th, 16th, and 17th holes.

Parnevik and Clarke Cracked

At the 17th, he sunk the ten-foot putt he needed to birdie this 223-yard hole: it was a very special moment in golf history. All the spectators willed Leonard to get a birdie. He seemed so sure of himself, gaining momentum throughout the day. This twenty-five-year-old player seemed to be invincible. Certainly Swede Jesper Parnevik and Irishman Darren Clarke had succumbed to the pressure, but Leonard still had a long way to go to blow the competition out of the water. Justin Leonard made that leap without emotion, keeping his cool to the end. The Scots no doubt dubbed him another "Wee Ice-Mon" as they huddled around the 18th green. To his credit, there are very few players of his age who would be capable of captivating and delighting a crowd as Palmer and Ballesteros have done.

A Remarkable Speech

Brad Faxon, Billy Andrade, Steve Stricker, and David Duval—almost of all of them as young as Leonard—dashed over to the green to congratulate him on his performance. He was the fifth American winner after Palmer in 1962, Weiskopf in 1973, Watson in 1982, and Calcavecchia in 1989—following the victories of John Daly and Tom Lehman. When Tom Kite learned at the airport that Leonard had upset the predictions, he canceled his flight and came back to congratulate Justin with the words: "Welcome to the team!" Leonard would become part of the Ryder Cup legend. When he was officially awarded the Claret Jug, Justin said a few words to the waiting crowd. He had something to say about everyone, beginning with his greatest opponents—Parnevik and Clarke—and including his match partner, Fred Couples. He went on to mention his family and friends back in Austin, Texas, whom he would have loved to witness his victory. With his generosity and consideration, Justin Leonard won his second victory of the day, gaining the public's approval. In the future, he could count on an army of European fans, delighted by the pleasant personality of this young man who is as shy as he is talented. Although he is a killer on the course, this twenty-five-year-old bachelor remains a gentleman elsewhere. In 1996, Cosmopolitan named him one of the 25 most eligible bachelors in the world.

A Hungry Shark in Search of a Major

The more important a competition, the more Leonard smells victory, and the more dangerous he becomes. He feeds on the situation and grows more powerful as the tension mounts. Without being like Greg Norman, Leonard can be compared to a shark, with his hunting instincts sharpened whenever he smells blood. Justin Leonard is a predator with an arsenal of weapons, such as his icy calm and his deadly putting. He came second in the U.S. PGA played at Winged Foot, and it was only the great Davis Love III who stopped him from winning a second Major in a row, a feat achieved by Nick Price in 1994. That is all he needed. This second place, added to all his other achievements, has made Leonard the best player in the Majors in 1997. His record shows clearly that Leonard has set some significant goals and that he has the mental and technical resources to achieve them.

TIGER

WOODS

TIGER WOODS

BORN DECEMBER 30, 1975
IN CYPRESS, CALIFORNIA

UNMARRIED

1 MAJOR
MASTERS 1997

7 PRO WINS

RYDER CUP 1997

LIVES IN ORLANDO, FLA

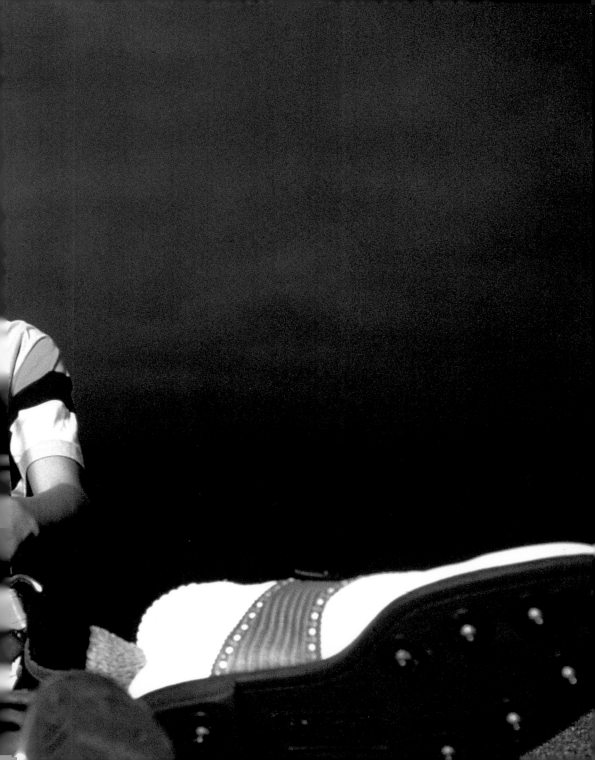

MOTHER AND SON: THE SAME SMILE

Kultida is happy and proud of her only son.

The angel for which American golf had waited for so long has materialized in the shape of a tiger. Young, handsome, smiling, all-powerful, Eldrick Tiger Woods is the first non-white hero to become a legend in his lifetime, a golf champion at the age of 21. In 1996, Tiger shot to the pinnacle of fame by smashing all records for someone of his age. The following year, Tiger showed he wasn't a nine-day wonder by winning the Masters, the first Major of the year and the first in a career, which was about as promising as is possible. The Tiger Woods phenomenon hit the headlines worldwide and demonstrated the incredible dynamism of the U.S. golfing scene. The American golfing authorities profited from this meteoric rise in that the sport gained interest for an ever wider and more diverse public. The PGA Tour has won financial support from advertisers and television networks, all of whom want to extend their sphere of influence. The young Woods has become a sort of "messiah" for them, preaching the gospel of golf. The future lies beyond the frontiers of the United States, where the whole world will be affected. Golf has the potential to become the favored sport of the 21st century, thanks to its universal spokesperson.

So American and yet So International
While serving in Vietnam, Earl Woods, an officer in the Green Berets, became a close friend of Lieutenant Colonel Ngyuen Phong, nicknamed Tiger for his bravery during

AGED 14, AT THE CYPRESS GOLF CLUB

(Preceding pages) *This was when the kid was more willing to be photographed.*

A POWERFUL SHOT

His secret is an amazingly fast turn on the descent.

EARL WOODS

He has devoted the second half of his life entirely to his son.

"The angel heralded by his father is as superhuman as Nicklaus was in his day."

RYDER CUP, VALDERRAMA, SEPTEMBER, 1997

(Facing) *Woods's debut but by no means the finest moment in his short career…*

the Vietnam War. The two men lost contact, but one event indirectly linked the two friends. Earl later met and married a young woman called Kultida in Thailand; in memory of his friend, he named their son "Tiger." Kultida wanted him to have the official first name of Eldrick. The name is clearly symbolic, combining the "e" of Earl and the "k" of Kultida, showing that his parents would always be with him. Woods was born in Cypress, California, on December 30, 1975. On his mother's side he has Thai, European, and Chinese blood, and through his father he inherited African and Native American blood! His father's words are unequivocal: "This young man has been chosen by God to bring more humanity into the world."

A Precociously Gifted Child

Ever since Earl Woods first put a club in his son's hands, the Tiger phenomenon hit the headlines. When he was only two years old, Bob Hope invited him onto the "Mike Douglas Show" to make his television debut, demonstrating his putting. Three years later, he made another television appearance, this time on "That's Incredible." At the age of three, Tiger played nine holes on the U.S. Naval G.C. at Cypress and shot a 48. Before he was 14 years old, he had won the Optimist International Junior World championship five times. In 1991, he became the youngest ever player to win the USGA's National Junior Championship. He won it again the following year. In 1993, after winning his third Junior title, he accepted a scholarship to Stanford University. Woods won his first victory in the U.S. Amateur at Sawgrass; yet again, at the age of 18, he was the youngest winner ever. He was

also the first to win this title three times in a row. The 1996 championship was played at the Pumpkin Ridge Golf Club and Tiger carried off the trophy, after lagging behind by five holes, finally winning at the 38th hole. He turned pro that August.

A Brilliant Finale to 1996, Continued the Following Year

Eldrick Woods won the amazing sum of $790,594, thanks to two wins, the Las Vegas Invitational and the Walt Disney World Classic, and by finishing in the Top Five, twice. This prize money and his 24th ranking in the Order of Merit meant he was able to bypass the heats for scorecards on the Tour. He stayed in top form, with four wins on the U.S. Tour, one Major, and an all-time record for prize-money—$2,066,833. At the age of 21, he had become the most powerful and the most accurate player in the world, achieving this at an earlier age than anyone before him.

A Record Number of Masters

"With his length and precision, this kid will win the Masters more than ten times," prophesied Jack Nicklaus in early 1997. In one crazy week, Tiger managed to destroy the previous record set by Severiano Ballesteros, who was 23 years and three days when he won it in 1980. By doing so in only 270 shots (70-66-65-69), he also beat Nicklaus's record (271) for the total number of shots played over four rounds. The 12 shots between Woods' score and that of Tom Kite, were the widest margin ever recorded in the history of the Tournament.

AN AMAZING SERIES OF AMATEUR WINS

His burning ambition to be a winner burst onto the U.S. Amateur scene in 1994.

HIS CADDY, MIKE "FLUFF" COWAN, A CUNNING FOX ON THE TOUR

His help was vital for Woods to win his first Masters.

A Teenage Idol

Tiger Woods has looks, success, money, and a fairy tale career in which he represents the American dream. Young people of all backgrounds worship him. Tiger's empire has become boundless, starting with his finances. At the age of 20, the young man had more than $60 million in the bank, thanks mainly to his long-term advertising contracts. Of his 1997 earnings of $26,100,000 (sixth in the Forbes ratings), $24 million alone came from commercial earnings.

The Other Side of the Coin

Tiger Woods has turned into the world-class golfer his father promised. The creation of his foundation represents the philanthropic side of his nature. Yet the future may

TIGER…

With his famous sock.

209

WITH BUTCH HARMON

The coach on Woods's team.

be a heavy burden for him to shoulder. Tiger cannot go anywhere unaccompanied and is under constant pressure. However, on the up-side, he is surrounded by people to help him manage his career. Mike "Fluff" Cowan is his caddie, Jay Brunza his sports psychologist, Hugh Norton is his agent and John Merchant is his lawyer, while Butch Harmon takes care of his fantastic swing. Tiger will have to learn to manage the mental and physical stresses that accompany his meteoric rise in order to maintain his exceptional career over time.

THE MISSED EAGLE AT THE 18TH ON PEBBLE BEACH

This putt followed a 265-yard shot using a No. 3 wood!

U.S. OPEN 1997, THE CONGRESSIONAL

Victory was denied him, although many people had been hoping for a repeat performance of Augusta.

KITE CAN BEAR WITNESS

Ryder Cup experience wasn't built in a day...

THE FIRST TEE: THE WORLD GOLF FOUNDATION'S NEW PROGRAM

The World Golf Foundation aims to promote golf to young people everywhere, advise public bodies, and help manage public courses of all sizes. Each project is a partnership between the public and private sectors. The men behind this action are Tim Finchem, director of the U.S. Tour, and Earl Woods, Tiger's father, acting in the name of the foundation created by his son. The aim is to put golf within the reach of every young person, regardless of social or economic background. According to the statistics, only two percent of young Americans aged from 12 through 19 have access to the sport.

"Since golf fosters values that can prove important in life—respect for others and for oneself—discovering and playing golf is a good experience for anyone. Golf could also become an important factor in racial integration (currently only three percent of golfers are black and two percent Hispanic). Golf can teach many lessons in life and open many doors." These are the words of ex-President George Bush, sponsor of the campaign.

The resources placed at the Foundation's disposal are in line with the importance of the organizations that have joined this great initiative, which is also supported by Tom Watson and Pat Bradley on behalf of the Tours. The partners are: PGA of America, the LPGA, the PGA Tour, the Tiger Woods Foundation, the Augusta National Golf Club, the World Golf Village, the National Golf Foundation, the American Society of Golf Course Architects, the Golf Course Superintendents Association of America, the American Junior Golf Foundation, the National Minority Golf Association, and the National Association of Junior Golfers.

A PROMISING AMATEUR RECORD

Three wins in a row in the U.S. Open Amateur. Here he is at Pumpkin Ridge in 1996.

A HISTORIC MASTERS

(Above) *Augusta, Sunday April 13, 1997: every record was broken.*

THE TIGER LEAPS TO VICTORY

(Facing) *The best players in the world were incapable of beating young Woods.*

WOMEN'S GOLF

Some background

Golf was born in the British Isles at a time of accepted male-domination. Combined with the fact that the game was developed by the freemasons, it is no surprise that it took 300 years from the time Mary Queen of Scots played a round of golf until the first women's clubs were created in 1867. Since it was out of the question for women to be allowed to join existing clubs, they had to create their own, as was the case in St. Andrews in 1867 and at Westward Ho! in 1868, when the North Devon Ladies Golf Club was founded. The sport became increasingly popular for women, and by the end of the century there were 30 women's clubs. It should be noted that 250 years after the invention of golf, several prestigious clubs, including the Royal St. George's, Augusta, and others, still do not admit women as members. This typically Anglo-Saxon form of ostracism does not exist in the rest of Europe, nor in the majority of clubs in the United States.

The First Lady Champions

In 1893, the British Ladies Amateur Championship was born, an example the United States followed two years later. These tournaments were created at the same time as their

CECILE LEITH

One of the earliest "grandes dames" of golf.

respective associations, the Ladies Golf Union and the Ladies Golf Association. Dorothy Campbell of North Berwick, on the Scottish Borders was one of the first women to venture over to the United States to play, but she was not the only woman golfer to attract attention. In a match designed to determine the best British amateur of either sex, Cecile Leith defeated Harold Hilton at Walton Heath in 1910. The die had been cast. The other ladies' champion of the 1920s was an English-woman named Joyce Wethered. Bob Jones would say she was the top amateur golfer of either sex. In the United States, Alexa Sterling, a childhood friend of Jones, who, like Jones, was born in Atlanta, found a redoubtable opponent in Glenna Collet Vare. Vare's fame has been perpetuated in the Vare Trophy, awarded for the lowest scoring average on the Women's Professional Tour.

Women's Pro Golf

The comparison between the two Tours is disconcerting. The difference between the situation on either side of the Atlantic has been most striking in the late 1990s. Europe's Order of Merit includes no more than five tournaments, while the American Tour consists of 34, with a total of $30 million in annual prize-money—twelve times

BABE ZAHARIAS IN 1946

From the Olympic Games to the greens of the U.S. Women's Open, Babe was an all-round sportswoman.

JAN STEPHENSON
This Australian golfer attracted much media attention on the women's circuit.

the sum offered by the Europeans. Far from the case in Europe, there are five million-dollar tournaments alone on the U.S. golfing calendar. Like its male alter ego, the LPGA Tour is very active in charity tournaments; from 1981 through 1995, the Tour brought in $78 million for charity! Women's golf is now attracting media attention and in 1997, 31 contests were televised. (The first televised competition was the U.S. Open in 1963, but it was not until 1982 that the four matches of the Nabisco Dinah Shore were given complete coverage.)

Champions who Made the Tour Famous

Mildred Didrikson was the first woman to show that women's golf was a sport in its own right. This young woman, better known as Babe Zaharias, first rose to sporting fame on the Olympic Games track in 1932. Her golfing career included wins in two amateur championships (1946 and 1947) and later, as a woman pro, three victories at the U.S. Open (1948, 1950, and 1954). Other champions of the day were Louise Suggs, Marylinn Smith, and Betsy Rawls. During the 1960s, Kathy Withworth had the most outstanding record; over the course of the decade she won 53 of 88 titles, making her the biggest winner of all time in women's golf.

Three Stars Born in the Seventies

From the 1975 Tour onward, the fame of professionals such as Ray Volpe, Judy Rankin, Joanne Carner, and Nancy Lopez spread beyond the little-publicized world of women's golf. Two other personalities dominated the sport, those of Amy Alcott and Jan Stephenson.

Alcott was the first to break through the $2 million prize-money barrier and Stephenson, who was born in Sydney, Australia, even won herself a male audience, including photographers and TV cameramen. Stephenson's good looks were as much of an attraction as her great play. Jan would later be the first woman to win a million dollars in prizemoney, but she was also the first woman golf course designer. The strong personalities of Lopez and Stephenson were to inspire the newcomers of the eighties—Beth Daniel, Betsy King, Patty Sheehan, and Pat Bradley.

The European Women Pros
It wasn't until the late eighties that some young women professionals came to the public's attention on the faltering European WPGA Tour. The Frenchwoman Marie-Laure De Lorenzi, the Englishwoman Laura Davies, and the Swede Liselotte Neumann were the first women pros whose performance heralded better days to come. Unfortunately, their circuit was in poor health and the U.S. Tour held much greater attractions. The European Tour has never managed to keep its champions at home. Even if women players turn in spectacular performances, the money and fame rarely follow. As a result, aspiring European women golfers often go to study at American universities and then spend a year or two on the European circuit before finally opting for the American Tour. The first European women to place in the Top Ten on American lists were the British players Alison Nicholas, Patricia Johnson, and Laura Davies, the Italian Stefania Croce, the Belgian Florence Descampe, and the Swedes Catrin Nilsmark, Liselotte Neumann, and Helen Alfredsson, though not all of them took the university route.

The New Generation
Nancy Lopez has been playing since the seventies and is thus a veteran of women's golf worldwide. Her successors will probably be American and Swedish. Annika Sorenstam represents the new generation of women golfers, as does Kelly Robbins. This new wave demonstrates elegance and style both on and off the course, as Jan Stephenson, Beth Boozer, and Laura Baugh did in their time. While the men will be playing on a world circuit from 1999 onward, the U.S. circuit has itself become a women's world tour. By emigrating to the United States, South African, European, and even Japanese women have found an environment which will enable their careers to flourish.

BETSY KING AT DALMAHOY, SCOTLAND

Flying the flag in the 1992 Solheim Cup.

The Future Lies in the U.S.

As in the case of the men, the women's circuit needs a favorable economic climate in which to develop. Beyond Japan and the United States, other countries do not have the potential pool of up-and-coming women players, nor sufficient commercial growth to attract enough sponsors to support a regular, firmly-based, circuit. The American LPGA Tour has set a high standard with its $30 million in annual prize-mone, which means it would be unlikely for another tour to come along and steal the women champions from the U.S. circuit. In the future, the same logic is likely to apply to the men as well. The question remains: Is the current direction of the women's game paving the way for all golf?

Nancy Lopez

NANCY LOPEZ

BORN JUNE 1, 1957
IN TORRANCE, CALIFORNIA

MARRIED, 3 CHILDREN

HALL OF FAME 1987

BOBBY JONES AWARD 1998

48 PRO WINS

SOLHEIM CUP 1990

LIVES IN ALBANY, GEORGIA

BALANCE

Inheriting the style of her father, a gifted amateur player.

Nancy Lopez had a whirlwind start to her professional career. Her first two years as a pro (1977–1978) heralded the dawn of a new era. Like Palmer and Ballesteros, Lopez was to become the center of attention. Nancy combined exceptional talent and charm. She caught the public's eye with great performances and her smile. Like all the greatest champions, she has demonstrated efficiency and determination: she has an unquenchable thirst for victory. Even at the age of 40, with 48 victories behind her, she is still determined to reach 50 victories. After more than 20 years on the Tour, Nancy Lopez remains among the Top Ten.

Her Father's Influence

When Nancy was only eight years old, her father chose to give his daughter the gift of a four-wood. This club became the first love of her life. She never failed to accompany her father, a talented amateur player himself, on the rough-and-ready course in

A SUPERB FINISH

Nancy makes sure that everything she starts is taken by her to a successful conclusion.

LOPEZ CONCENTRATING ON HER GAME

She has drawn much media attention to Women's Golf.

Roswell, New Mexico. Her father, Domingo, would be her teacher and coach throughout her career. He soon realized that his daughter had a great talent for the sport. Domingo taught Nancy never to be afraid: she feared nothing and no one, and proved it by becoming the women's amateur champion of New Mexico at the age of 12! This performance would be followed by many more during the eight years of her amateur career. She was twice USGA Junior Girls champion, and she won the Western Open and the Mexican Open.

A Spectacular Start to her Career

Her five victories in a row in 1978 left no doubt as to the talent of this future women's champion. Domingo taught her well: "I owe it to him that I rarely leave the fairways because he told me that the roughs at Roswell were off limits. In fact, they were fields of pebbles which were unplayable." Nancy Lopez's reign began in 1979 with eight victories. There was a period during which she was semi-retired for three reasons: her children Ashley Marie, Erinn Shea, and Torri Heather, born respectively in 1983, 1986, and 1991. Nancy's parents played a leading role at the beginning of her career; later the support and balance of her husband and children were just as important. In 1982, she married baseball star Ray Knight, her second marriage.

Her Swing and the Hall of Fame

Nancy has an empirical style—there is nothing classic about it. She learned from her father an unusual swing with a sort of loop at the top. "Technique is not important to me—I need to find the right movement even under pressure while keeping all of my sense of touch and feel," she explains. Her slow backswing enables her to accelerate quickly as the club comes through the ball. "The mental part is what motivates me. I am a very positive person." That is certainly one of the keys to her success and her victories which, in 1987, brought her into the small group of women golfers who meet the criteria of the Hall of Fame. Thanks to her win in the Sarasota Classic, the 35th of her career, Nancy made it into that inner circle. Strangely, it was this same Sarasota Classic that marked Nancy's first win ten years earlier, a victory she dedicated to her mother who died of peritonitis in 1977.

A Fresh Start at 40

Nancy practiced constantly at the beginning of her career, and her subsequent decision to focus on family life singularly complicated her goal of making a fresh start after having children. "Of course, I don't aim to repeat the nine wins I had in my first season, but I feel just as young as my opponents." Nancy Lopez has always admitted that after starting a family she never managed to put all her energy into the game. Her challenge was to combine family life and competitive golf and she was sure she would succeed. "I decided to lose weight to be ready physically. My mind doesn't worry me. It becomes stronger with age."

Member of an Ethnic Minority

Just as Tiger Woods boasts of being an African American, Nancy Lopez is proud of her Mexican American heritage. The discrimination she suffered as a teenager has left its mark. Her parents, her religious faith, and her family life have helped her through difficult times. She does not allow anyone else to raise and care for her children. "I'll teach my daughter to cook and run a home just as I shall teach her to be respected as a woman." Nancy Lopez has always proved she has an iron will and a great deal of moral courage, especially at the worst times, such as her divorce from her first husband in 1981, or her mother's death in 1977. Her performance and her natural charm were great assets for the Women's Tour, and Nancy was a great draw for sponsors, as Tiger Woods would be 20 years later.

The Bob Jones Award 1998

Nancy has just been awarded the most prestigious distinction by the USGA, the Bob Jones Award. Her sportsmanship, generosity, grace, and sporting prowess have made her a worthy recipient. Nancy was very touched to be awarded this distinction in January 1998, just as she was re-starting her career: "This honor is an even greater incentive to win the U.S. Women's Open, which I have never won before. I feel myself to be even stronger." Lopez is a worthy successor to such talents as Francis Ouimet, Babe Zaharias, Ben Hogan, Jack Nicklaus, and Gene Sarazen. She is the ninth woman to win the award, preceded by Mildred D. Zaharias, Margaret Curtis, Patty Berg, Glenna Collet Vare, Maureen Garrett, Peggy Kirk Bell, and Betsy Rawls.

At the age of 40, having won countless prizes, distinctions, and awards, Nancy Lopez has returned to the circuit in her quest for the elusive U.S. Women's Open, which she desperately wants to win. One thing is certain: even without this victory, Nancy will keep smiling and continue to work hard for the profession which has given her so much pleasure.

"My swing is no uglier than Arnold Palmer's and it's the same ugly swing every time."

Finally winning the U.S. Women's Open.

ANNIKA SORENSTAM

EFFICIENCY

A straightforward swing and a carefully calculated strategy.

When a young woman makes her mark quickly on the professional circuit, she is automatically compared to Nancy Lopez. Conditions are certainly different now that there are so many good women players on the American Women's Tour. The competition is much tougher, but there has never been so much prize money in women's golf. A woman golfer can earn more than a million dollars a year! To reach that position, Annika Sorenstam decided as a teenager to attend an American university, because in Europe it is not possible to combine sport and study.

The American and Swedish Connections

Like many Swedes, Annika's father was a sportsman, and he loved teaching his daughter. Sorenstam senior soon realized that Annika had great determination. She wanted to win everything she played, whether it was chess, cards, or golf, which she had been playing since the age of 12 at the Bro Balsta Club north of Stockholm. Annika was lucky enough to meet Pia Nilsson, the Swedish women's national team coach. Nilsson's greatest strength lies in her ability to combine fun with learning. She spotted Annika's raw talent and the young girl proved to be a fast learner. In 1988, in agreement with Annika's own pro (Henri Reis), her parents, and the Swedish Federation, Annika took the big step of enrolling at the University of Arizona.

The Big Step

Through university competitions, Annika developed and refined her natural swing and inspired putting. In 1991, she was named Woman Player of the Year and became a member of the NCAA All-American team. The next year she produced an even more extraordinary succession of top-quality performances. She finished first in the Amateur World Championships and second in the U.S. Amateur. With her seven university victories and performances in the U.S. Open, Annika turned pro in 1993.

Her First Season in Europe

Annika was unknown on the European circuit, and thus surprised everyone in the Amateur World Championships. Her preparation and poise won her the distinction of Rookie of the Year on the European Tour. She was also one of the first women to play with Callaway clubs. From her base at the Wigwam Resort in Arizona, Annika returned to competitive golf in late 1993 when she joined the American Tour. Again, she won the Rookie of the Year title, since it was her first appearance in the U.S., and even managed to finish three matches in the Top Ten. She greatly enjoys the Tour because the greens are fast, enabling her to demonstrate her exceptional putting skills.

1995—A Year of Dedication

After three victories, Annika had the luxury of finishing at the top of the final Order of Merit rankings and winning $666,533 in prize money in 1995. More titles followed. She was the first foreign player to win the Vare Trophy for the lowest average score and was nominated Athlete of the Year in Sweden. This meteoric rise has much in common with that of Lopez, such as the simplicity of her swing, which remains consistent even under pressure, and the effectiveness of her short game. This helps her win where others show signs of weakness. She had her first two European victories,

---

A WOMEN'S GOLFING LEGEND

(Previous page) *Annika has been No. 1 in the world ever since she became a pro.*

including the famous Hennessy Cup this year. In 14 out of 20 tournaments, Sorenstam has been among the Top Ten—irrefutable proof of her excellent play. She won the U.S. Open again at Pine Needles Golf Club; only six women have ever managed to do so two years running. Betsy King was the last to do it in 1989–1990 but Annika is the first non-American to have reached such heights. While she now has $808,311 in prize money to her credit, Australian Karie Webb was the first to break the million-dollar mark and win the top ranking in the Order of Merit. She only played in two or three European Tournaments, but won the Trygg Hansa Ladies Open in Sweden in 1966.

The Surprise of the U.S. Women's Open in 1997

In January 1997, Annika Sorenstam married David Esch. The season started off well, but the golfing world asked itself whether the Swedish champion would be able to win the most prestigious of the women's Majors for the third time. The press applied pressure and the newspaper headlines emphasized the intensity of the competition— no one had ever won three U.S. Opens in a row. Disaster struck and Annika did not even make the cut on the Pumpkin Ridge course. "I don't understand what happened. I putted very badly. I must have been too nervous." Sorenstam fought on, determined to stay in the tournament which was won by the Scotswoman, Alison Nicholas. She later regained her confidence, and went on to win several more competitions, ending the season with six victories and a record in the Order of Merit with $1,236,789 in prize money!

Lessons to be Drawn

While all this confirms her international supremacy in the world of golf, Annika has decided to organize the season differently in order to avoid exhaustion. The best woman player in the world needs to do a lot of practicing but in the future, she will only play two or three tournaments in a row, so as to be able to retain all of her "punch" and dynamism. Maturity and balance are Sorenstam's most important assets, enabling her to forget her poor shots and concentrate on the rest of the round. Even off the course, her wit and charm ensure that this young European champion has a bright future ahead of her.

BRITISH LADIES OPEN 1995, WOBURN

When can we expect a major European victory to round off her achievements so far?

ANNIKA SORENSTAM

BORN OCTOBER 9, 1970
IN STOCKHOLM, SWEDEN

MARRIED

U.S. WOMEN'S OPEN
1995-96

18 PRO WINS

SOLHEIM CUP 1994-96

LIVES IN INCLINE VILLAGE,
NEVADA
AND STOCKHOLM, SWEDEN

THE LEGENDARY COURSES

"God designed the golf courses; golf architects only discover them."

The earliest golf courses (St. Andrews, Dornoch, North Berwick, Prestwick) are so well-adapted to the needs of the sport that they are indubitably the inspiration for the architects of today. A golf course designer has to create a course that challenges the skill and versatility of the player. First he must find a suitable site. The best and most interesting shot is generally one to the green. Take the second shot at the 17th at St. Andrews; the 12th hole, par three at Augusta; or the 16th hole at Cypress Point overlooking the ocean. All these holes epitomize good golf course design, combining features that make the game interesting and challenging. When studying a new site, the best architects start by defining the par-three holes. Since these are the shortest holes, they must compress the elements golfers are looking for. In fact, the par-threes ought be the favored spots, but unfortunately this is rarely the case.

ST. ANDREWS, THE 2ND AND 3RD

This course has often been compared to a lunar landscape.

American architects are masters at the transformation and remodeling of the land, applying a fertile imagination to the huge resources they are able to mobilize. Every location is by no means suitable for the development of a course with the charm and soul of those created by, for example, Donald Ross (the architect of Seminole and Pinehurst). Despite extensive alterations and sophisticated construction techniques, the raw natural landscape predominates. The sea, ancient trees, mountains, dunes, a river, heather, groves, lakes, are all elements which contribute to the design of a beautiful course. In golf, the concept of the "beauty of the course" has as much to do with the quality of the shot to be played as the beauty of the landscape or even how a course is maintained. When these three elements are combined, the results are the legendary courses which have shaped the sport today.

Augusta National Golf Club
Tree-Nursery and Orchard

The Berghmans family came from Ghent in Belgium and settled in Augusta, Georgia, to start a nursery, where they planned to grow ornamental plants and fruit trees. The business did not do well and they decided to sell it. Bob Jones, having ended his career in competition golf, learned of the property and went to visit it. As a native of Atlanta, Jones was familiar with the region and the city of Augusta. He fell in love with the place and each time he visited, and started to picture the layout of the holes. Having fallen under its spell, he began to mobilize the

TICKETS FOR THE MATCH

(Facing page) *It's tough trying to get tickets, except for the oldtimers!*

AUGUSTA NATIONAL GOLF CLUB

(Preceding pages) *Gene Sarazen sends the Masters into orbit at the 15th hole.*

funds he needed. To help him, he brought in Clifford Roberts, a New York banker who had influence in the White House. They had two goals, namely to create a private club for the use of a few hand-picked members, and to build a course that would be capable of hosting the greatest professional players of the day.

A Club in the South for the Northern Elite

The idea was sound and they had no trouble at all in getting enough members interested in playing in the pleasant climate of Georgia: in New York, where most had their businesses, climatic conditions did not favor golfing. The members came from all over the country, though there were never more than 300 of them at any one time. In the 1930s, when the economy was in such bad shape, bankers, lawyers, judges, and businessmen wanted to meet somewhere discreet. The private golf club is very reminiscent of the freemasons' lodge where members would gather for secret meetings. In order to meet the

AUGUSTA, AMEN CORNER

So many dramas have been played over these 155 yards…   243

criteria required for the course to be suitable for championship play, Jones called in Alister Mackenzie, who had just finished creating Cypress Point on the Monterey Peninsula in California.

These two men did what every architect should do: play golf over rough country to discover the best and most appropriate shots. Since the course was intended to host the greatest players in the United States, the greens needed special attention. The two associates understood each other perfectly and shared the same vision for the course. They played the course over and over while it was under construction and fine-tuned it. Unfortunately, Mackenzie died in 1934, at the age of 64, without seeing his masterpiece completed. After three years of development, the course hosted its first competition, the same year Mackenzie passed away. The following year, the two nine-hole loops were reversed, the first hole becoming the tenth and vice versa. When the second competition was held at Augusta in 1935, one player attracted media attention to this event and the unusual course. On his second shot at the 15th (par five), Gene Sarazen produced an albatross with a magnificent four-wood shot. The next day, he won the 36-hole playoff (the first and last 36-hole playoff). The Augusta Masters became a legend.

Bob Jones's Inestimable Legacy

Bob Jones, creator of Augusta, left golfers a tremendous legacy. He has no equal in Continental Europe. Severiano Ballesteros is the only player who has contributed to his own country, Spain, and to Europe as a whole, that individual genius which has proved so important in the development of the game. Golf needs individuals to guide and inspire, men like Old Tom Morris, his son Young Tom, Allan Robertson, and Willie Park, Jr. These pioneers spent their lives trying to understand the game, playing it, and later finding the best course locations. They are responsible for laying the foundations of the great modern game of golf.

Breathtaking Natural Beauty

More than 35 greenskeepers work full time to conquer the elements and create the smoothest green lawns at Augusta. The most modern techniques are studied and applied. For example, after extensive research, it was found that bentgrass could be

RAE'S CREEK GUARDS ACCESS TO THE 13TH HOLE

Don't allow yourself to be distracted by the beauty of the surroundings.

replaced effectively by Bermuda grass on the greens and this was done in October, 1980. The Augusta Committee makes a change to the course every year. It is determined that the club shall remain one of the leading facilities and keep abreast of any advances in the sport. A pond was created at the 16th by Robert Trent Jones to increase the tension at the last holes. This remodeling dates only from the mid-1980s. Jones witnessed changes at the 10th green and at the 11th, where Hogan decided he would never make the green in two shots. The original 22 sand traps have grown to around 50. Nicklaus believes the number of sand traps needs to be increased because big hitters can drive the ball over them. Since the course has no rough except the wooded areas, the fairways have had to be altered. Woods had too many opportunities to hit wedge shots during that fantastic tournament in April 1997, when he broke all records and won his first Masters.

THE SWILCAN BURN BRIDGE

An ancient witness to the development of the game of golf.

The Amen Corner

The 11th, 12th, and the 13th (also known as the Amen Corner) are the most famous holes because the public has seen so much of them. Tommy Nakajima took a 13 at the 13th (a par-five), and Tom Weiskopf produced the same score when playing Augusta's shortest hole, the 12th. The river that winds around the holes presents quite a few problems. Rae's Creek has been responsible for a number of defeats, as Curtis Strange can testify from his game against Bernhard Langer in 1985. The water barriers have defined Augusta's history. Sarazen put the cat among the pigeons in 1935 when he hit the ball with a four-wood into the water feature at the 15th, and in 1986 Ballesteros displayed weakness under pressure for the first time by using a four-iron to send the ball right into the middle of the pond. Augusta is in a wonderful location. The many different flowers and scents from the trees contribute to the majesty of the place. The colors are enchanting; camellias, magnolias, rhododendrons, and azaleas constantly remind you that you are in a Bob Jones heaven.

Augusta's Nine Par Three Holes

The Augusta members decided to create nine holes whose par was three in order to devise an agreeable course that would demand long shots. Before the tournament begins, all the players are invited to play a match over nine holes of the famous course. Legend has it that a player who wins this competition will never manage to win the Masters that year. But that's not the only strange story about this section of the course. During one of these competitions, a member spoke to Clifford Roberts and remarked that the two sand traps behind the green didn't seem to have much point to them. "On the other hand," he continued, "if a little hillock was put there, the public would get a better view." The next year, Roberts handed the person who had made the suggestion a note on which he had written: "Cost of construction to remove the sand traps and create a hillock. You had a great idea there, pal!" The pal's name was Jackson Stephens and he later became president of the club. The story goes that Dwight D. Eisenhower, the only American president to have been a member at Augusta, is buried somewhere under the course he loved so much. There is a tree at the 14th tee which still bears his name because he always managed to hit it with his ball. Despite numerous requests, it seems the committee will never agree to remove it.

ST. ANDREWS

(Preceding pages) *The city, university, hedge, tidewater, and the Old Course, between the Jubilee and the New Course.*

The Old Course at St. Andrews
The Old Course Sees its Destiny as Part of that of the R&A

Even if golf was not exactly invented here, many refinements have taken place at this very special spot. Three of the game's most important assets owe their origin to St. Andrews: the popularity of the sport, the inspiration for the shape of the course, and the rules of the game. After all, people have enjoyed hitting a ball with a stick for centuries, but here, on the east coast of Scotland, there was a social consensus for promoting practice on communal land in such a way as to open the game up to all. Games were free at St. Andrews until 1913! Even today, the courses are managed equally by the city and by the Royal and Ancient Golf Club (the R&A). Several clubs share the courses, none having exclusive use. In practice, any golfer, from whatever social and economic background, has the right to reserve a tee at St. Andrews. That certainly does not apply to the majority of prestigious courses available exclusively for the pleasure of their wealthy members and, where applicable, the pros on the Tour. On Sundays in March, the course is closed to golfers to allow walkers access to the course (the course is no longer closed on Sundays to observe the Lord's Day, as was once the case) and for maintenance and repairs. Each year, about 42,000 rounds of golf are played over the Old Course. The waiting-list is often as long as six months!

An Architectural Gem

It so happens that the golf course is also a magnificent piece of architecture. The topography, the natural contours, the clumps of broom, the roughs, the Swilcan Burn, the nearness of the sea, the sand-dunes, and the low drystone walls are all features which make the course so interesting for golfers and course designers alike. Two predominant features have inspired contemporary designers. The greens, and the approaches to them, have been naturally modeled with great subtlety. An approach shot to the green has to be carefully considered, otherwise the next approach shot or putt will be difficult. There are several solutions, but only a few are effective. There is the option of choosing the most direct route to the greens or going the long way around in order to avoid sand traps, the rough, and out-of-bounds areas. St. Andrews inspired the first golf course architects such as Old Tom Morris (the first pro appointed to St. Andrews) and Willie Park, Jr., both of whom were among the

THE 17TH HOLE AT ST. ANDREWS

The Road Hole Bunker.

The whole scene is impressive—the road, the off-limits, the low wall, and the famous clubhouse.

first to preach the gospel of golf. Having gained all their experience on the Old Course, the pioneers of course design chose locations that would provide as much interest in the game as St. Andrews—as much flexibility in situating the greens and a diversity of shots to be played, varying the length of holes and the arrangement of the obstacles. These architects had the good sense to copy the spirit of St. Andrews and not just its outward appearance. For the short holes, the par-threes, they took care to make the shot challenging and were not interested in the number of par-threes, since there are only two of them on the Old Course.

St. Andrews also gave birth to men who were deeply attached to the sport and took on the responsibility of defining the rules. From 1897 until the rules and their interpretation became a joint effort with the USGA, the R&A was the sole authority for defining how the game was played (setting 18 holes as the standard course length, for example). Several clubs use the course, including the R&A which has 1,800 members based at the handsome clubhouse built in 1854. Half of these members come from abroad; the only way to become a member is to be introduced by another member. To illustrate the esteem in which the R&A and the Old Course are held, from 1919 onward all the clubs hosting the British Open have left the organization of the championship entirely in their hands.

Ben Hogan and St. Andrews

Hogan is the only champion never to have played the Old Course, for unknown reasons. Certainly the Texan did everything he could to fulfill his great passion in life: to succeed at golf. Hogan had a deep psychological motivation. His traumatic early experiences and the mental torment of his father may explain this. One thing is certain, he was a man of very unusual character, taciturn and ironic. His determination and energy drove him on day and night, from sunrise to sunset. Hogan was haunted. Since St. Andrews could do nothing for his career, it can be supposed that he saw no reason to test himself on the Old Course, even out of curiosity. Ben was a careerist rather than someone who liked a challenge, in contrast to Bobby Jones who displayed a deep affection for the Old Course. In 1956, Jones was granted the keys to the city of St. Andrews and was honored to see his name given to the tenth hole.

A Piece of Advice for Playing the Old Course: Aim Left

The course has changed over the years and has benefited from the experience of the best players. From the original five holes, it was extended first to 12 holes, then, in 1754, to 22. A decade later, the best golfers of the period suggested that the first four outward bound holes should be combined (as well as the last four inward bound holes, which were clearly too short), to reduce the course to 18 holes with nine double greens. Then in 1842, the course was reversed, so that it is now played from right to left with seven double greens and four single greens (the latter at holes 1, 9, 17, and 18). When teeing off, it is best to aim to the left of the flag. This makes it possible to avoid the numerous sand traps hidden in folds of the fairway. Experience is the watchword at St. Andrews. Approach shots to the green are always hard to judge, especially as the flagpole is not always visible, due to the undulations of the dunes.

Nicklaus won two of his British Opens at St. Andrews. Since Jack was so brilliant at course management, leaving little to chance, he had a huge advantage over the other players. St. Andrews, like Muirfield, always chooses its champions from among the keenest players. Ballesteros and Faldo have demonstrated that the Old Course is one which requires a lot of careful thought and attention, and demands much skill and careful shotmaking ability. It is a perfect test of golfing skills.

Pebble Beach

Pebble Beach is one of the greatest attractions of the Monterey Peninsula in the Bay of Carmel. Samuel F. B. Morse, President of the Pacific Improvement Company of Monterey (a real estate development company) and a descendant of the inventor of telegraphy, asked one of his employees to build a golf course along the famous 17-Mile Drive. The choice of employee was by no means random. Jack Neville, a member of his sales force, had been amateur champion of the state of California in both 1912 and 1913. As a champion player from the age of 17, Jack was precocious and gifted in golf course design. He planned the course routing and got help in the drawing and location of the bunkers from Douglas Grant, another California champion. In 1919, the Pebble Beach Golf Links was opened to the public, and has remained public ever since. John Francis Neville (Jack's full name) remained an employee of the real estate development company all his life. He also helped create a few designs in collaboration with other architects and pursued a brilliant sporting career, winning the State championship in 1919, 1922, and 1929. He reached the peak of his career in 1914 when he won the Northwest Pacific championship, and again when he was selected to play in the 1923 Walker Cup. Right up until his death in 1978 at the age of 83, the management of the course asked his advice each time any alteration was made to the layout.

Neville, Mackenzie, and Hunter

In their book *The Golf Course*, Cornish and Whitten explain that for many years Pebble Beach was known as the "Del Monte Golf Club," since the Del Monte Hotel was located near the course. When the Bay of Carmel is swept by a fierce wind, the seven holes which face the ocean become monstrously difficult to play. Here again there is evidence of Neville's genius. As the designer of a neighboring course, Alister

THE 9TH HOLE AT PEBBLE BEACH

An architectural gem in a breathtaking natural setting.

Mackenzie was asked to make a few changes to the course in cooperation with Robert Hunter. Hunter was a famous professor of sociology at Berkeley, best known for his campaign against child labor. In 1926, this golfing fanatic who had studied in London wrote an essay on a very pertinent subject, entitled "The Links." The story goes that Hunter brought Mackenzie to California and to Cypress Point. The two men became close friends and collaborated on several projects, including Green Hills, Mill Brae, Meadox, Fairfax, Pittsburgh, Valley C, and Northwood. A third associate later joined the pair. He was H. Chandler Egan, whom Neville had beaten in 1914 for the Northwest Pacific title.

Nicklaus, Watson, and Kite
These are the names of the three winners of the U.S. Open championships organized on the Pebble Beach links. Only the greatest golfers can meet the challenge this

course presents. The best players prefer difficult courses with excellent, rolling, fast greens which are very rewarding. Pebble Beach leaves nothing to chance. Nicklaus's victory in 1972 was repeated in 1982 before Watson hit an almost impossible approach shot to achieve a birdie on the 17th, one of the most difficult par-three holes in the world. Pebble Beach will be hosting the Open in 2000.

It is here that Tom Kite finally made it, having waited until his forty-second year to enter his name in the roll of honor of Grand Slam winners. Fortunately, Pebble Beach was waiting for him. His consistency and his excellent short game are a joy to behold. This, the first year in which Montgomerie decided to show his face at a U.S. Open, was a tough one, as the fierce wind made the links hellishly difficult to play on the last afternoon of the tournament. Kite played perfectly, however, and won the contest with two strokes to spare, thus lifting a huge weight off his shoulders.

The sadly missed Dave Marr, who became the U.S. PGA champion in 1965, spoke of "the beauty of the grandeur of Pebble Beach." If the ocean and the rocky cliffs combine to create a magnificent backdrop to the location, the 7th, 8th, 9th, and 10th holes can do a lot of damage to a player's scorecard. These holes, which are considered to be the four hardest on the Tour, also inspired Lee Trevino, who considered the 6th to be "the perfect hole for committing suicide." If Nicklaus had a tough time accepting Watson's birdie at the 17th, especially as Watson had hooked his first shot, he admitted that Pebble Beach was the course he would choose if there was only one course left to play.

Cypress Point

Cypress Point is a neighbor of Pebble Beach, and overlooks the Bay of Carmel one hundred miles south of San Francisco. This course has the wildest, most magnificent scenery of any course in the United States—maybe in the world. It is shorter, and thus less competitive than its alter ego, but Cypress Point is considered to be the "Sistine Chapel of Golf" (to quote former President of the USGA, Sandy Tatum). Its three most spectacular holes, the 15th, 16th, and 17th, are considered to be both architectural and scenic gems. The course is situated on the most beautiful part of the Monterey Peninsula. The cliffs fall dramatically away to the sea, where the blue-and-white waters swirl around detached rocks, creating the impression that the Pacific Ocean is

PEBBLE BEACH: THE IMPRESSIVE, 120-YARD 7TH HOLE

(Preceding pages) *A memorable occasion for anyone lucky enough to make it to the green.*

GOLF AND OCEAN

Payne Stewart in 1991 at Pebble Beach, on the Monterey Peninsula.

boiling. The course, designed by Alister Mackenzie, opened in 1928. It is one which shows extraordinary respect for its surroundings. Together with Robert Hunter and Jack Fleming, a longtime collaborator, Mackenzie invested all his knowledge and experience into its design.

The architects used every feature they could think of to enrich the 18 holes. The ocean, dunes, cypress trees, heather, and cliffs create a backdrop which ranges from pleasant to spectacular. The 16th hole is the most photographed hole in the world with its 200-yard spread along the Pacific clifftop. Bing Crosby actually achieved a hole-in-one in 1947. What a souvenir! A feat like that would be enough to make a golfer think he had a brilliant future. No one can fail to be moved by the magnificence of the course, though it can be cruel when there is a high wind. "The beauty and the beast," as Jack Lemmon has nicknamed it, is owned exclusively by 250 members, unlike its publicly owned neighbor.

PINE VALLEY

A wonderful course with a fascinating and exceptionally demanding layout.

At Last—A Woman in This World Which Is so Much a Man's

Bob Jones also fell under the spell of this course, which he visited for the first time in 1929 after being eliminated from the first round of the U.S. Open at Pebble Beach. This was the day on which Jones decided to appoint Mackenzie to build his next project: Augusta. The design for Cypress was originally awarded to Seth Raynor (who created the Monterey Peninsula Country Club), but he died soon after presenting his original rough drawings, which were never used. It was Marion Hollins, one of the few women who feature in the very macho history of Cypress, who, under the influence of Robert Hunter, hired the Scottish architect to take over the project. Finally, a women was admitted into the ranks of the golf decision makers. Her start was not easy, however. As a result of the Great Depression, she had a great deal of difficulty finding members—there were only 50 at the start. Happily, given the startling beauty of the course, the situation could only improve.

Pine Valley

Pine Valley is often described as the best course in the world. The Irishman Joe Carr is one of those who considers this course at Clementon, New Jersey, to be the "ultimate." It is representative of the style of golf course architecture that preceded the strategic period. Like many others of its generation, the course is built on sandy soil covered with pine forest. The course designer was not a professional, although he was assisted by Harry Colt after 1913. George Crump was a wealthy hotel owner who made his dream come true by building his own golf course, designing and financing it personally.

The huge deforestation project and Crump's death in 1918 delayed the opening of the first 18 holes until 1919. The financial and architectural assistance of the Wilson Brothers from Merion were needed to complete the task. For a golfer, there is only one possible way to play this course, and that is to keep the ball on the fairway. Each shot needs to be directed with surgical precision; otherwise the ball will be trapped by one of the innumerable obstacles. Heaven is green in Pine Valley, the green of the fairways and the greens, but hell is yellow, like the sand in the traps or in the roughs, or blue like the waters of the lakes sprinkled around the course, including the one by the 15th tee, a par-five hole of 600 yards. The par-three holes are gems and are typical of the essential attraction of this course, the quality of the shots needed to reach the flag. Pine Valley is one of those courses that every potential golf course architect ought to study from all angles. The questions to be asked are: why is it so beautiful; why have the greens been located where they are; what makes it so big; is the course dishonest or unfair? The wrong response would be to make courses more difficult by adding lots of sand traps, shortening the fairways, and adding lots of water obstacles. Pleasure in the game involves much more subtle considerations. It is understood that this type of course would suit the best players. Even if the course is not suitable for Tour competitions (there is no room for spectators), many of the best players come to this legendary site, including the Walker Cup competitors in 1985.

Royal Melbourne

Royal Melbourne has always held an important place because it is the material proof that a golf course can be noteworthy without being on British or American soil. The course is laid out to take advantage of existing contours and scenery without the need

for massive earthworks. Golf can be exciting and challenging even when it is not sophisticated. The course consists of two 18-hole routes which cover a seaside and heathland landscape. Ben Crenshaw, one of the professionals who is the most knowledgeable about the history of the sport and its architecture, is one of the greatest fans of the Royal Melbourne course. No doubt this is because the Texan is one of the best putters of all time and perfectly understands the subtlety of the design of the greens and the positioning of the flags.

This course, like Augusta, has to be played with an eye to the green. In relation to the position of the flag, a very precise spot on the fairway should be selected; otherwise reaching the green would be very difficult. A successful player needs to be good at shotmaking and follow-through, emulating Ben Hogan, who adored this course. As for the sand traps, they blend beautifully into the greens like waves on the sea. Here again, one needs to be adept at the game in order not to fall into their snares. With the exception of the par-three holes, all the holes are dog legs, intensifying the degree of difficulty. The Royal Melbourne has always been the pride of the Australian professionals on the tour—Norman Von Nida, Ken Nagle, Peter Thomson, Roger Davis, and Greg Norman.

THE 15TH HOLE AT PINE VALLEY

(Preceding pages) *Perhaps the most difficult course in the world—you dare not leave the fairway.*

AN AERIAL VIEW OF THE ROYAL MELBOURNE

(Following pages) *A demonstration of the genius of Alister Mackenzie.*

ROYAL MELBOURNE, WEST COURSE

Its design includes an exceptionally large number of sand traps.

ALISTER MACKENZIE, FROM DOCTOR TO GOLF ARCHITECT

The son of Scottish parents, Alister Mackenzie was born in Normanton, Yorkshire, England, and was a brilliant student at Cambridge, where he studied medicine, natural history, and chemistry. He practiced medicine during the Boer War in South Africa and continued to do so upon his return to Leeds. In 1907, Harry Colt, an excellent golfer and golf architect, was staying with him, and was very impressed with Mackenzie's designs for the greens at the new course to be built at Alwoodley near Leeds. He suggested that Mackenzie help him in his work and in 1909, Mackenzie abandoned medicine for his new passion. In 1914, he won a postal competition to design a hole at Lido Long Island Country Club, his first stepping-stone to recognition. Then came World War I, and Mackenzie turned his attention to camouflage, a subject in which he excelled since he knew exactly how to use the features of the landscape to their best advantage. His technique was inspired by the Boers in South Africa whom he encountered during his first experiences of war. Indeed it was through camouflage, rather than through medicine, that he is credited with saving thousands of lives during the war. Again thanks to Colt and his partner, Charles Alison, Alister went to the United States in 1918 and also built courses in Australia, Argentina, New Zealand, Uruguay, Scotland, Ireland, and England. In 1920, he published his 13 commandments for golf architecture, still considered to be the golden rules for course design.

THE RYDER CUP

Though Samuel Ryder, a wealthy English seed merchant who sold his products by mail order, didn't discover golf until he was 50, he became the founder of the greatest competition in the golfing calendar. Ryder was born in the north of England and worked at his father's business in Sale, Cheshire, but later moved south to St. Albans for his health. Ryder had a lot of time to spend on his favorite leisure activity and had a hole built at his home. He became a scratch (handicap 0) player in five years thanks to his personal tutor, Abe Mitchell. Ryder accompanied Mitchell to many competitions and was particularly enthralled by a 1926 match at Wentworth between players from both sides of the Atlantic. Mitchell beat Jim Barnes (who had won the British Open) by eight and seven. Ryder greatly admired the American competitors who had traveled five days by sea to test themselves on a British course against British players, and decided that the experiment should be repeated.

THE RYDER CUP TROPHY

The much-coveted prize…

In 1926, Sam Ryder invited professional golfers to compete for prize money that he was offering. The champions who responded included Ted Ray, Walter Hagen, Tommy Armour, and George Duncan. Since this match was played in Europe, the British traveled to the United States the next year to play for the Cup just before the U.S. Open. Unfortunately, Abe Mitchell had to leave the ship with appendicitis just before it sailed and missed the trip, as did Ryder. Over in the U.S., at Worcester, Mass., it was decided that the tournament be played every two years, on alternate sides of the Atlantic. The gold Cup donated by Ryder, topped with the statuette of a golfer representing Abe Mitchell, was first played for in 1927 and became a big hit.

The Continent Joins In

In 1979, the British PGA agreed to change the format of the competition, which they had been allowed to organize since 1934. Garrido and Ballesteros were thus brought onto the British team. Once again, the initiative had come from the champions. Europe finally won the cup, at the Belfry in 1985, and broke the string of 13 consecutive defeats.

A MUST IN EVERY PROFESSIONAL GOLFER'S CAREER

Presenting the Ryder Cup teams in 1997 (Europe, on the left; the United States, above).

Major Changes in the Formula

From the original 12, the number of matches was increased to 24 in 1961, 32 after the 1963 event, 20 points (one point per match) in 1977, and 28 points in 1979. The 1981 format seems to work best and is still in use. It consists of 16 double rounds (divided into foursomes and twosomes) and 12 single rounds. All the games are match plays, there are no playoffs. Each win scores one point and in the event of a draw, half a point is awarded to each side.

Selection is made on the Order of Merit rankings but each team captain has the right to choose two of his players. In 1996, Ballesteros proposed that the choice be extended to four players. The reason, he said, was that the best team possible needed to be selected and that several European players had produced their best scores on the American Tour, which did not enable them to chalk up points in the European rankings.

One formula which remains unchanged is the prize. The Ryder Cup is the only competition in which pro champions do not play for money. Only their expenses are reimbursed. However, since Europe joined in 1985, the tournament has become so

important, the respective PGAs gain millions of dollars in television rights, entrance fees, and merchandising. Mark O'Meara and Tiger Woods have said that they felt exploited by the organizers of the Ryder Cup. Not all the players agree, and some even consider that the competition is a fair way for the pros to pay some money back into their professional associations.

Valderrama, a Major First

On three occasions from 1985 through 1993, the British PGA hosted the matches played in Europe at its new headquarters at the Belfry. Peter Alliss and Dave Thomas designed the course so that it could comfortably hold a large number of spectators and television crews. If the 10th and 18th holes have caused a lot of ink to be spilled, it cannot be said that the rest of the course has aroused great enthusiasm, since the natural setting is rather uninteresting. In recognition of the large number of points won by the Spanish players, the PGA awarded the captaincy to Ballesteros. Valderrama was chosen for the 1997 Ryder Cup, a course designed by Robert Trent Jones, which has hosted the Volvo Masters for the last nine years and is one of the most beautiful and competitive courses in the game.

The Spanish, and Jaime Ortiz Patino in particular, president and owner of the club, proved their vitality and efficiency in their perfect organization of the Ryder Cup. The only sour note was the torrential rain that spoiled several of the matches. Ballesteros and Kite, the two captains, made their confrontation one of the most exciting of all the matches ever played in the Cup, but there was a great spirit of fair play throughout. The Belfry, jealous of its position and eager to become home to the European end of the tournament once again, will be hosting the Ryder Cup in 2001. The Cup will hit Ireland in 2005.

A World-Class Event

The Ryder Cup certainly made golf into a media sport thanks to its telegenic qualities. The tournament is perfect for those who love to watch golf, whether they play or not. The suspense and beautiful scenery make it one of the most anticipated events in the sport, thanks to the support of Nicklaus and Ballesteros. The greatest moments in the cup have usually occurred when these two players take center stage. In 1969, at

1987: A HISTORIC YEAR

(Preceding pages) *The first-ever European victory on American soil.*

RAYMOND FLOYD, THE BELFRY 1989

One of a long line of great captains—Hagen, Hogen, Snead, Nelson, Palmer, Nicklaus, Watson, etc.

Royal Birkdale, Nicklaus gave a three-foot putt at the 18th against Tony Jacklin, giving both teams an absolutely equal score of 16-16. Jack had this to say on the last green: "I don't think you'll miss it, Tony, but anyway I'm not going to give you the opportunity." Ballesteros also played memorable matches. His most famous feat was performed in 1983 against Fuzzy Zoeller, thanks to a legendary three-wood played from a bunker. Nicklaus later said, "That was the greatest shot I ever got the chance to see." Though the shot didn't bring Europe victory, it was of supreme importance. After the match, Seve went up to Tony Jacklin, the Captain, and told him: "This time, we know we can beat them. Next time we'll win, I can feel it!"

Ryder Cup Pressure

The tension is so great during these matches that a player's nerve can go at any moment. The honor of two continents is at stake and this, combined with the exceptional media presence generating millions of spectators, makes players wonder if they can keep their

Year	Location	Teams	Points		
1927	Worcester, Massachusetts	U.S.A.	9.5	G.B.	2.5
1929	Moortown, England	G.B.	7	U.S.A.	5
1931	Columbus, Ohio	U.S.A.	9	G.B.	3
1933	Southport, England	G.B.	6.5	U.S.A.	5.5
1935	Ridgewood, New Jersey	U.S.A.	9	G.B.	3
1937	Southport, England	U.S.A.	8	G.B.	4
1947	Portland, Oregon	U.S.A.	11	G.B.	1
1949	Scarborough, England	U.S.A.	7	G.B.	5
1951	Pinehurst, North Carolina	U.S.A.	9.5	G.B.	2
1953	Wentworth, England	U.S.A.	6.5	G.B.	5.5
1955	Palm Springs, California	U.S.A.	8	G.B.	4
1957	Yorkshire, England	G.B.	7.5	U.S.A.	4
1959	Palm Desert, California	U.S.A.	8.5	G.B.	3
1961	St. Anne's-On-Sea, England	U.S.A.	14.5	G.B.	9
1963	Atlanta, Georgia	U.S.A.	23	G.B.	9
1965	Southport, England	U.S.A.	19.5	G.B.	12
1967	Houston, Texas	U.S.A.	23.5	G.B.	8
1969	Southport, England	U.S.A.	16	G.B.	16 (*)
1971	St. Louis, Louisiana	U.S.A.	18.5	G.B.	13
1973	Muirfield, Scotland	U.S.A.	19	G.B. and Ireland	13
1975	Ligioner, Pennsylvania	U.S.A.	21	G.B. and Ireland	11
1977	St. Anne's-On-Sea, England	U.S.A.	12.5	G.B. and Ireland	7
1979	White Sulfur Springs, West Virginia	U.S.A.	17	Europe	11
1981	Surrey, England	U.S.A.	18.5	Europe	9
1983	Palm Beach Gardens, Florida	U.S.A.	14.5	Europe	13
1985	Sutton Coldfield, England	Europe	16.5	U.S.A.	11
1987	Dublin, Ohio	Europe	15	U.S.A.	13
1989	Sutton Coldfield, England	U.S.A.	14	Europe	14 (**)
1991	Kiawah Island, South Carolina	U.S.A.	14.5	Europe	13.5
1993	Sutton Coldfield, England	U.S.A.	15	Europe	13
1995	Rochester, New York	Europe	14.5	U.S.A.	13.5
1997	Valderrama, Spain	Europe	14	U.S.A.	13

(*) A draw: The United States retained the Ryder Cup.

(**) A draw: Europe retained the Ryder Cup.

1939-1945: the Ryder Cup match was not played (World War II).

THE BUILD OF A CHAMPION

In the ring, George Forman became a star! (November, 1994).

cool. The giant screens dotted over the course are constant reminders of the ever-present TV cameras. There is always the danger of a competitor reaching the point where he is no longer able to manage the sheer level of stress. The Ryder Cup has reached such a fever pitch that only medical resources can enable players to repair the damage caused by all that adrenaline. Tranquilizers, homeopathy, beta-blockers, and many other methods have been used to help overcome the pressure. Maybe it's time to think seriously about taking some of the pressure off. But since the professional golfing organizations gain most from the huge money-spinning opportunities of the tournament, they are hardly likely to want to kill the goose that lays the golden eggs, nor will they ban the medication that makes it possible to bear the consequences of this global spectacle.

GLOSSARY

Address: stance adopted by the golfer who is preparing to hit the ball. The rules of golf frequently refer to this precise moment. (e.g., a ball which moves after having been addressed.)

Albatross: scoring three below par. This means two shots when par is five.

Approach: the last shot before the green. The term is generally applied to shots of less than 100 yards. An approach shot can also be played with a putter when outside the green; this is called the Texas Wedge. Some examples of an approach are a rolling approach (a chip shot or a pitch-and-run), a lobbed approach, and a shot from a sand trap.

Bermuda Grass and bentgrass: types of grasses planted on greens.

Birdie: a score on a hole of one shot below par.

Caddy: the word comes from the French "cadet," a young man. Caddies used just to carry clubs for a player, but they soon became indispensable counselors to competition golfers. Until the early 20th century, players were allowed more than 14 clubs.

Clubhouse: building containing the locker rooms, offices, pro shop, bar, and restaurant.

Course: a golf course usually has 18 holes.

Cut: selection process based on stroke play after two days of competition in a tournament consisting of four rounds. The cut is generally fixed at the first 75 competitors out of 150 entrants. Only players who have passed the cut can play for the prize money.

Dog leg: a description of holes that cannot be played in a straight line. Generally, in a dog leg par-four, the first part of the hole lines up with the tee, and then after the "turning point" the line of the shot swivels to the right or left. Where par is five, the dog leg may be double.

Draw: the trajectory of a ball that finishes its flight from right to left (hook).

Driving range: area set aside for hitting practice drives and for practicing the swing.

Eagle: score of two shots below par for a hole.

Fade: the trajectory of a ball that finishes its flight from left to right (slice).

Fairway: the wide path of smoothly trimmed grass as designated in the rules of golf. The tee, fairways, and greens are areas where the ball is safe, whereas roughs, water barriers, and sand traps are there to guide the player and punish those whose shots are too ambitious or erratic. Fairway grass is cut to between 3/4 and one inch.

Featherie: ball used in the earliest stages of the game. The featherie was made of a top hat full of goose or duck feathers boiled down and pushed inside a sheepskin or calfskin sheath.

Fine-tuning: golf course design expression referring to making adjustments, adding finishing touches, and retouching the contours of the greens before they are seeded with grass.

Green: the site of the hole and flag, consisting of a very smoothly trimmed lawn, the grass being 1/8 to 1/4 inch high. The average green covers 500 sq. yards and is never completely flat, the differences of level between ball and hole constituting the putting line.

Greenkeeper: person responsible for course maintenance. Also known as the head gardener.

Gutta percha: natural resin from a tropical tree used to make balls in the second half of the 19th century. Gutta percha replaced the featherie and was later replaced by the Haskell.

Hickory: a supple North American white wood (related to the walnut) used for golf club shafts until the 1930s. Hickory was replaced by metal until the advent of graphite. Hickory had a certain amount of torque, which always caused good swingers to hook the ball.

Hole in one: when a ball hit from the tee goes straight into the hole. This can occur at par-three holes but rarely at par-four holes.

Hook: to hook the ball means to hit it in such a way as to give it a right-to-left bias.

Links: golf courses along seashores were given this name because they consisted of a number of grass-covered surfaces interspersed with sand-dunes like the links in a chain.

Major: the four events in the Grand Slam. In date order, they are the Masters at Augusta in April, the U.S. Open in June, the British Open in July, and the U.S. PGA in August.

Niblick: old name for the number nine-iron.

Off limits: each course has clearly defined limits. Any ball found beyond them is considered to be off limits and must be abandoned for playing the hole. Rule 27 defines the procedures.

Par: the number of shots fixed for a hole at a particular course. Par is calculated by allowing two shots on the greens, plus an additional shot for holes shorter than 230 yards (par three = three shots), two additional shots for holes of between 200 and 450 yards (par four), and three additional shots for holes longer than 400 yards. Depending on the configuration of the course, holes of between 400 and 450 yards are considered to be par four or five. These distances apply to lengths for men. For women, the distances for calculating par are reduced by 15 percent.

Pitching wedge: a club with a lift of about 50°. This club is used for shots of less than 100 yards and for approach shots. Tiger Woods uses his pitching wedge for much longer shots.

PGA: Professional Golfers' Association. There is a difference between associations of tournament players (PGA Tour, PGA European Tour) and associations of golf instructors (PGA in England, APGF in France).

PGA Tour, PGA European Tour: The circuit professionals tour in the U.S. or Europe.

Playoff: a group of shots played over one or more holes where two or more players have finished equal after playing the round.

Practice: practice putts and shots executed to practice swinging. They are performed without a ball.

Prize money: the sum of money awarded to players in a competition. Each circuit has its own formula for awarding the amounts. As a general rule, only players who have made the cut receive a share of the prize money equal to their place in the classification.

Pro-Am: competition format in which a professional golfer plays alongside one or more amateurs, making a team. These teams play against each other. As a general rule, each professional tournament is preceded by a Pro-Am. These competitions give sponsors and officials the opportunity to play with a pro, while the pro gets to familiarize himself with the layout of the course and make contact with the organizers of the tournament.

Pro shop: store in or near the clubhouse, usually run by the pro, selling golfing equipment.

Putt: a golf stroke produced using a putter, usually on the greens. The par for each hole is calculated by allowing for at least two putts a hole.

Putter: a club designed to propel the ball without raising it from the ground, for use on the greens. The rules of golf govern the specifications for a putter. The term "putter" also applies to a person who is putting.

Resort: a golfing resort is a complex which consists of hotel and catering facilities and one or more courses, as well as other sporting and leisure facilities, such as tennis courts, swimming pool, gym, beach, children's play area, etc.

Rough: any part of the course which is not a fairway, a green, hazards, or an obstacle. The term is applied mainly to grassy areas where the grass is not cut short (the latter being the fairway). Rough may consist of grass of any length, even grass which is never cut.

Round: a round of golf consists of playing all 18 holes; half a round means nine holes.

Routing: architectural term referring to the positioning of a hole in relation to the others. The routing plan is the first drawing produced by an architect when designing a course.

Sand trap: the sand trap, also known as a bunker, is a sunken pit of sand designed to penalize erratic shots by trapping them in this difficult surface. Sand traps are usually located around greens, and have to be gotten out of by using a sand wedge, a club with a heavy heel angled in such a way as to give the ball the lift it needs to bounce out of the trap. Sand traps are important factors to be taken into account when analyzing playing strategy at a hole.

Sand wedge: a club with a weighted heel angled so as to make the ball jump elegantly out of the sand trap. The striking surface of the club is pitched at an angle of 54° to 60°. The sand wedge or wedge can also be used outside of sand traps for short approach shots, such as lobs.

Slice: trajectory of a ball from left to right.

Swing: movement of the body, hands, and arms which moves the club through the air in a swinging motion so that it hits the ball squarely. When a driver is being used, the head of the club may cover a total distance of 15 yards during the movement.

Tee: term used to denote the starting point of a hole, which consists of a small square of ground, often slightly raised from the surrounding area. The ball is placed on a tiny wooden or plastic T-shaped pedestal, also known as a tee. Taking this first shot at a hole is known as "teeing off." Courses now have two sets of teeing-off points, men's and ladies', the ladies' tee being 15 percent closer to the hole than the men's tee.

USGA: United States Golf Association. The American equivalent of St. Andrews as regards the rules of golf. The association governs the amateur game in the United States.

Walker Cup: this is the equivalent of the Ryder Cup for male amateur players and is played every two years. Since 1922, the Walker Cup has been a match between an American team and a team of players drawn from Ireland and Great Britain. Eight competitors in each camp play 24 matches, 12 foursomes, and eight twosomes.

Water hazard: any kind of water obstruction such as a stream, pond, lake, canal, or other body of water as defined by the club. Water obstacles are also known as water obstacles and are marked with pickets or yellow lines. Where these obstacles are alongside the fairway they are marked in red. See rule 26.

AWARDS

THE OPEN GOLF CHAMPIONSHIP

Year	Winner	Location	Score
1860	Willie Park	Prestwick	174
1861	Tom Morris, Sr.	Prestwick	163
1862	Tom Morris, Sr.	Prestwick	163
1863	Willie Park	Prestwick	168
1864	Tom Morris, Sr.	Prestwick	160
1865	Andrew Strath	Prestwick	162
1866	Willie Park	Prestwick	169
1867	Tom Morris, Sr.	Prestwick	170
1868	Tom Morris, Jr.	Prestwick	157
1869	Tom Morris, Jr.	Prestwick	154
1870	Tom Morris, Jr.	Prestwick	149
1872	Tom Morris, Jr.	Prestwick	166
1873	Tom Kidd	St. Andrews	179
1874	Mungo Park	Musselburgh	159
1875	Willie Park	Prestwick	166
1876	Bob Martin	St. Andrews	176
1877	Jamie Anderson	Musselburgh	160
1878	Jamie Anderson	Prestwick	157
1879	Jamie Anderson	St. Andrews	169
1880	Robert Ferguson	Musselburgh	162
1881	Robert Ferguson	Prestwick	170
1882	Robert Ferguson	St. Andrews	171
1883	Willie Fernie *	Musselburgh	159
1884	Jack Simpson	Prestwick	160
1885	Bob Martin	St. Andrews	171
1886	David Brown	Musselburgh	157
1887	Willie Park, Jr.	Prestwick	161
1888	Jack Burns	St. Andrews	171
1889	Willie Park, Jr. *	Musselburgh	155
1890	John Ball (AM)	Prestwick	164
1891	Hugh Kirkaldy	St. Andrews	166
1892	Harold H. Hilton	Muirfield	305
1893	W. Auchterlonie	Prestwick	322
1894	John H. Taylor	Sandwich	326
1895	John H. Taylor	St. Andrews	322
1896	Harry Vardon*	Muirfield	316
1897	Harold H. Hilton	Hoylake	314
1898	Harry Vardon	Prestwick	307
1899	Harry Vardon	Sandwich	310
1900	John H. Taylor	St. Andrews	309
1901	James Braid	Muirfield	309
1902	Alexander Herd	Hoylake	307
1903	Harry Vardon	Prestwick	300
1904	Jack White	Sandwich	296
1905	James Braid	St. Andrews	318
1906	James Braid	Muirfield	300
1907	Arnaud Massy	Hoylake	312
1908	James Braid	Prestwick	291
1909	John H. Taylor	Deal	295
1910	James Braid	St. Andrews	299
1911	Harry Vardon*	Sandwich	303
1912	Edward Ray	Muirfield	295
1913	John H. Taylor	Hoylake	304
1914	Harry Vardon	Prestwick	306
1920	George Duncan	Deal	303
1921	Jock Hutchison*	St. Andrews	296
1922	Walter Hagen	Sandwich	300
1923	Arthur Havers	Troon	295
1924	Walter Hagen	Hoylake	301
1925	James Barnes	Prestwick	300
1926	Robert T. Jones, Jr.	R^{al} Lytham & St. Anne's	291
1927	Robert T. Jones, Jr.	St. Andrews	285
1928	Walter Hagen	Sandwich	292

1929	Walter Hagen	Muirfield	292		1980	Tom Watson	Muirfield	271
1930	Robert T. Jones, Jr.	Hoylake	291		1981	Bill Rogers	Royal St. George's	276
1931	Tommy Armour	Carnoustie	296		1982	Tom Watson	Royal Troon	284
1932	Gene Sarazen	Prince's, Sandwich	283		1983	Tom Watson	Royal Birkdale	275
1933	Denny Shute*	St. Andrews	292		1984	Severiano Ballesteros	St. Andrews	276
1934	Henry Cotton	Sandwich	283		1985	Sandy Lyle	Royal St. George's	282
1935	Alfred Perry	Muirfield	283		1986	Greg Norman	Turnberry	280
1936	Alfred Padgham	Hoylake	287		1987	Nick Faldo	Muirfield	279
1937	Henry Cotton	Carnoustie	290		1988	Severiano Ballesteros	R^{al} Lytham & St. Anne's	273
1938	R. A. Whitcombe	Sandwich	295		1989	Mark Calcavecchia*	Royal Troon	275
1939	Richard Burton	St. Andrews	290		1990	Nick Faldo	St. Andrews	270
1946	Sam Snead	St. Andrews	290		1991	Ian Baker-Finch	Royal Birkdale	272
1947	Fred Daly	Hoylake	293		1992	Nick Faldo	Muirfield	272
1948	Henry Cotton	Muirfield	294		1993	Greg Norman	Royal St. George's	267
1949	Bobby Locke*	Royal St. George's	283		1994	Nick Price	Turnberry	268
1950	Bobby Locke	Troon	279		1995	John Daly*	St. Andrews	282
1951	Max Faulkner	Royal Portrus	285		1996	Tom Lehman	R^{al} Lytham & St. Anne's	271
1952	Bobby Locke	R^{al} Lytham & St. Anne's	287		1997	Justin Leonard	Royal Troon	272
1953	Ben Hogan	Carnoustie	282					
1954	Peter Thomson	Royal Birkdale	283					
1955	Peter Thomson	St. Andrews	281					
1956	Peter Thomson	Hoylake	286					
1957	Bobby Locke	St. Andrews	279					
1958	Peter Thomson*	R^{al} Lytham & St. Anne's	278					
1959	Gary Player	Muirfield	284					
1960	Ken Nagle	St. Andrews	278					
1961	Arnold Palmer	Royal Birkdale	284					
1962	Arnold Palmer	Troon	276					
1963	Bob Charles*	R^{al} Lytham & St. Anne's	277					
1964	Tony Lema	St. Andrews	279					
1965	Peter Thomson	Royal Birkdale	285					
1966	Jack Nicklaus	Muirfield	282					
1967	Roberto De Vicenzo	Hoylake	278					
1968	Gary Player	Carnoustie	289					
1969	Tony Jacklin	R^{al} Lytham & St. Anne's	280					
1970	Jack Nicklaus*	St. Andrews	283					
1971	Lee Trevino	Royal Birkdale	278					
1972	Lee Trevino	Muirfield	278					
1973	Tom Weiskopf	Troon	276					
1974	Gary Player	R^{al} Lytham & St. Anne's	282					
1975	Tom Watson*	Carnoustie	279					
1976	Johnny Miller	Royal Birkdale	279					
1977	Tom Watson	Turnberry	268					
1978	Jack Nicklaus	St. Andrews	281					
1979	Severiano Ballesteros	R^{al} Lytham & St. Anne's	283					

* Won after a playoff

1915–1919: the Open Golf Championship was not held (World War I)

1940–1945: the Open Golf Championship was not held (World War II)

U.S. MASTERS

Augusta National Golf Club, Augusta, Georgia

1934	Horton Smith	284
1935	Gene Sarazen	282
1936	Horton Smith	285
1937	Byron Nelson	283
1938	Henry Picard	285
1939	Ralph Guldahl	279
1940	Jimmy Demaret	280
1941	Craig Wood	280
1942	Byron Nelson*	280
1946	Herman Keiser	282
1947	Jimmy Demaret	281
1948	Claude Harmon	279
1949	Sam Snead	282
1950	Jimmy Demaret	283
1951	Ben Hogan	280
1952	Sam Snead	286
1953	Ben Hogan	274
1954	Sam Snead*	289
1955	Cary Middlecoff	279

AWARDS

Masters

Year	Winner	Score
1956	Jack Burke, Jr.	289
1957	Doug Ford	283
1958	Arnold Palmer	284
1959	Art Wall, Jr.	284
1960	Arnold Palmer	282
1961	Gary Player	280
1962	Arnold Palmer*	280
1963	Jack Nicklaus	286
1964	Arnold Palmer	276
1965	Jack Nicklaus	271
1966	Jack Nicklaus*	288
1967	Gay Brewer, Jr.	280
1968	Bob Goalby	277
1969	George Archer	281
1970	Billy Casper *	279
1971	Charles Coody	279
1972	Jack Nicklaus	286
1973	Tommy Aaron	283
1974	Gary Player	278
1975	Jack Nicklaus	276
1976	Ray Floyd	271
1977	Tom Watson	276
1978	Gary Player	277
1979	Fuzzy Zoeller*	280
1980	Severiano Ballesteros	275
1981	Tom Watson	280
1982	Craig Stadler*	284
1983	Severiano Ballesteros	280
1984	Ben Crenshaw	277
1985	Bernhard Langer	282
1986	Jack Nicklaus	279
1987	Larry Mize*	285
1988	Sandy Lyle	281
1989	Nick Faldo*	283
1990	Nick Faldo*	278
1991	Ian Woosnam	277
1992	Fred Couples	275
1993	Bernhard Langer	277
1994	José-Maria Olazábal	279
1995	Ben Crenshaw	274
1996	Nick Faldo	276
1997	Tiger Woods	270

*Won after a playoff

1943–1945 th U.S. Masters was not held (World War II)

U.S. OPEN CHAMPIONSHIP

Year	Winner	Location	Score
1895	Horace Rawlins	Newport	173 (36)
1896	James Foulis	Shinnecock Hills	152 (36)
1897	Joe Lloyd	Chicago	162 (36)
1898	Fred Herd	Myopia Hunt C.	328 (72)
1899	Willie Smith	Baltimore	315
1900	Harry Vardon	Chicago	313
1901	Willie Anderson*	Myopia Hunt C.	331
1902	Laurie Auchterlonie	Garden City	307
1903	Willie Anderson*	Baltusrol	307
1904	Willie Anderson	Glen View	303
1905	Willie Anderson	Myopia Hunt C.	314
1906	Alex Smith	Onwentsia Club	295
1907	Alex Ross	Philadelphia Cricket C.	302
1908	Fred McLeod*	Myopia Hunt C.	322
1909	George Sargent	Englewood	290
1910	Alex Smith*	Philadelphia Cricket C.	298
1911	John McDermott*	Chicago	307
1912	John McDermott	C. C. of Buffalo	294
1913	Francis Ouimet*	C. C., Brookline	304
1914	Walter Hagen	Midlothian	290
1915	Jerome Travers	Baltusrol	297
1916	Charles Evans, Jr.	Minikahda Club	286
1919	Walter Hagen*	Brae Burn	301
1920	Edward Ray	Inverness	295
1921	James M. Barnes	Columbia	289
1922	Gene Sarazen	Skokie	288
1923	Robert T. Jones, Jr.*	Inwood	296
1924	Cyril Walker	Oakland Hills	297
1925	W. MacFarlane*	Worcester	291
1926	Robert T. Jones, Jr.	Scioto	293
1927	Tommy Armour*	Oakmont	301
1928	Johnny Farrell*	Olympia Fields	294
1929	Robert T. Jones, Jr.	Winged Foot	294
1930	Robert T. Jones, Jr.	Interlachen	287
1931	Billy Burke*	Inverness Club	292
1932	Gene Sarazen	Fresh Meadows	286
1933	Johnny Goodman	North Shore	287
1934	Olin Dutra	Merion Cricket C.	293
1935	Sam Parks, Jr.	Oakmont	299
1936	Tony Manero	Baltusrol	282
1937	Ralph Guldahl	Oakland Hills	281
1938	Ralph Guldahl	Cherry Hills	284
1939	Byron Nelson*	Philadelphia	284

1940	Lawson Little*	Canterbury	287
1941	Craig Wood	Colonial Club	284
1946	Lloyd Mangrum*	Canterbury	284
1947	Lew Worsham*	St. Louis	282
1948	Ben Hogan	Riviera	276
1949	Carry Middlecoff	Medinah	286
1950	Ben Hogan*	Merion	287
1951	Ben Hogan	Oakland Hills	287
1952	Julius Boros	Northwood	281
1953	Ben Hogan	Oakmont	283
1954	Ed Furgol	Baltusrol	284
1955	Jack Fleck*	Olympic Club	287
1956	Carry Middlecoff	Oak Hill	281
1957	Dick Mayer*	Inverness Club	282
1958	Tommy Bolt	Southern Hills	283
1959	Billy Casper	Winged Foot	282
1960	Arnold Palmer	Cherry Hills	280
1961	Gene Littler	Oakland Hills	281
1962	Jack Nicklaus*	Oakmont	283
1963	Julius Boros*	C. C., Brookline	293
1964	Ken Venturi	Congressional	278
1965	Gary Player*	Bellerive	282
1966	Billy Casper*	Olympic Club	278
1967	Jack Nicklaus	Baltusrol	275
1968	Lee Trevino	Oak Hill	272
1969	Orville Moody	Champions G. C.	281
1970	Tony Jacklin	Hazeltine	281
1971	Lee Trevino*	Merion	280
1972	Jack Nicklaus	Pebble Beach	290
1973	Johnny Miller	Oakmont	279
1974	Hale Irwin	Southern Hills	287
1975	Lou Graham*	Medinah	287
1976	Jerry Pate	Atlantic Athletic C.	290
1977	Hubert Green	Southern Hills	278
1978	Andy North	Cherry Hills	285
1979	Hale Irwin	Inverness Club	284
1980	Jack Nicklaus	Baltusrol	272
1981	David Graham	Merion	273
1982	Tom Watson	Pebble Beach	282
1983	Larry Nelson	Oakmont	280
1984	Fuzzy Zoeller*	Southern Hills	276
1985	Andy North	Oakland Hills	279
1986	Ray Floyd	Shinnecock Hills	279
1987	Scott Simpson	Olympic Club	277
1988	Curtis Strange*	C. C., Brookline	278

1989	Curtis Strange	Oak Hill	278
1990	Hale Irwin	Medinah	280
1991	Payne Stewart	Hazeltine	282
1992	Tom Kite	Pebble Beach	285
1993	Lee Janzen	Baltusrol	272
1994	Ernie Els*	Oakmont	279
1995	Corey Pavin	Shinnecock Hills	280
1996	Steve Jones	Oakland Hills	278
1997	Ernie Els	Congressional	276

*Won after a playoff

1917–1918: the U.S. Open Championship was not held (World War I)

1942–1945: the U.S. Open Golf Championship was not held (World War II)

U.S. PGA CHAMPIONSHIP

1916	James Barnes	Siwanoy	1 hole
1919	James Barnes	Engineers C. C.	6 & 5
1920	Jock Hutchison	Flosmoor	1 hole
1921	Walter Hagen	Inwood	3 & 2
1922	Gene Sarazen	Oakmont	4 & 3
1923	Gene Sarazen	Pelham	1 hole (38)
1924	Walter Hagen	French Lick C. C.	2 holes
1925	Walter Hagen	Olympia Fields	6 & 5
1926	Walter Hagen	Salisbury	5 & 3
1927	Walter Hagen	Cedar Crest	1 hole
1928	Leo Diegel	Five Farms	6 & 5
1929	Leo Diegel	Hillcrest	6 & 4
1930	Tommy Armour	Fresh Meadows	1 hole
1931	Tom Creavy	Wannamoisett	2 & 1
1932	Olin Dutra	Keller	4 & 3
1933	Gene Sarazen	Blue Mound	5 & 4
1934	Paul Runyan	Park C. C.	1 hole (38)
1935	Johnny Revolta	Twin Hills	5 & 4
1936	Denny Shute	Pinehurst	3 & 2
1937	Denny Shute	Pittsburgh	1 hole (37)
1938	Paul Runyan	Shawnee	8 & 7
1939	Henry Picard	Pomonok	1 hole (37)
1940	Byron Nelson	Hershey	1 hole
1941	Vic Ghezzi	Cherry Hills	1 hole (38)
1942	Sam Snead	Seaview	2 & 1
1944	Bob Hamilton	Manito	1 hole
1945	Byron Nelson	Morraine	4 & 3
1946	Ben Hogan	Portland	6 & 4
1947	Jim Ferrier	Plum Hollow	2 & 1

1948	Ben Hogan	Norwood Hills	7 & 6
1949	Sam Snead	Hermitage	3 & 2
1950	Chandler Harper	Scioto	4 & 3
1951	Sam Snead	Oakmont	7 & 6
1952	Jim Turnesa	Big Spring	1 hole
1953	Walter Burkemo	Birmingham	2 & 1
1954	Chick Harbert	Keller	4 & 3
1955	Doug Ford	Meadowbrook	4 & 3
1956	Jack Burke	Blue Hill	3 & 2
1957	Lionel Hebert	Miami Valley	2 & 1
1958	Dow Finsterwald	Llanerch	276
1959	Bob Rosburg	Minneapolis	277
1960	Jay Hebert	Firestone	281
1961	Jerry Barber	Olympia Fields	277
1962	Gary Player	Aronomink	278
1963	Jack Nicklaus	Dallas Athletic C.	279
1964	Bobby Nichols	Columbus	271
1965	Dave Marr	Laurel Valley	280
1966	Al Geiberger	Firestone	280
1967	Don January*	Columbine	281
1968	Juluis Boros	Pecan Valley	281
1969	Ray Floyd	NCR C. C.	276
1970	Dave Stockton	Southern Hills	279
1971	Jack Nicklaus	PGA National	281
1972	Gary Player	Oakland Hills	281
1973	Jack Nicklaus	Canterbury	277
1974	Lee Trevino	Tanglewood	276
1975	Jack Nicklaus	Firestone	276
1976	Dave Stockton	Congressional C. C.	281
1977	Lanny Wadkins*	Pebble Beach	282
1978	John Mahaffey*	Oakmont	276
1979	David Graham*	Oakland Hills	272
1980	Jack Nicklaus	Oak Hill	274
1981	Larry Nelson	Atlanta Athletic C.	273
1982	Ray Floyd	Southern Hills	272
1983	Hal Sutton	Riviera	274
1984	Lee Trevino	Shoal Creek	273
1985	Hubert Green	Cherry Hills	278
1986	Bob Tway	Inverness	276
1987	Larry Nelson*	PGA National	287
1988	Jeff Sluman	Oak Tree C. C.	272
1989	Payne Stewart	Kemper Lakes	276
1990	Wayne Grady	Shoal Creek	282
1991	John Daly	Crooked Stick	276
1992	Nick Price	Bellerive	278
1993	Paul Azinger*	Inverness	272
1994	Nick Price	Southern Hills	269
1995	Steve Elkington*	Riviera C. C.	267
1996	Mark Brooks*	Valhalla	277
1997	Davis Love III	Winged Foot	269

* Won after a playoff

Until 1957, U.S. PGA Championship was fought on the number of holes.

1917–1918: U.S. PGA Championship not played (World War I).

1943: U.S. PGA Championship not played (World War II).

Photography © Vandystadt/Allsport:

Patrick Bertucelli – Nathan Bilow – Simon Bruty – Dave Cannon – Phil Cole – J. D. Cuban – Bob Daemmrich – Hulton Deutsch – A. Downie – Stephen Dunn – J. Durban – Matt Harris – Michael Hobbs – Rusty Jarret – Craig Jones – Art Kane – Ross Kinnaird – David Leah – Alan D. Levenson – Jean-Marc Loubat – Andy Lyons – Tim Matthews – Stephen Munday – Gary Newkirk – Mike Powell – Steve Powell – Gary M. Prior – Andrew Redington – David Rogers – Paul Severn – Dan Smith – Jamie Squire.

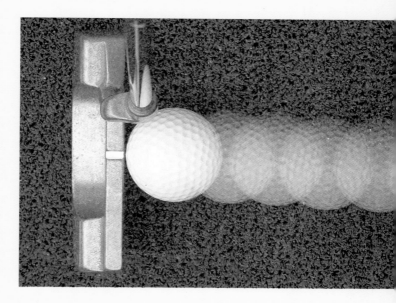

Bibliography

GREEN (Robert), *Golf, An Illustrated History of the Game*, London, Willow Books, Collins, 1987.

The Royal and Ancient Golf Club, *Golfers Handbook*, London, Macmillan Press Limited, 1992.

CORNISH (Geoffrey S.) and WHITTEN (Ronald E.), *The Golf Course*, New York, The Routledge Press, 1987.

British Broadcasting Corporation, *The World of Golf*, London, Gordon Menzies, BBC, 1982.

with the help of: Alliss, Ward-Thomas, Dobereiner, Goodner, Laidlaw, McDonnell, Mair, Menzies, and Williams.

PGA Tour, *Official Media Golf Guide of the PGA TOUR*, Ponte Vedra Beach (Florida), PGA TOUR, 1997.

European Tour, *The EUROPEAN TOUR Media Guide*, Wentworth, Surrey, PGA European Tour, 1997.

CARR (Steven) and STRUGNELL (Sally), *The Complete Book of Golf*, New York, Barnes and Noble Inc., 1993.

Acknowledgments

The author would like to thank everyone who contributed to the publication of this book:

Martine Assouline for her faith in me,

Valérie Ledent, Jacques Temmerman, Patrick Lebon, Paolo Leonardi, and Robert Low for their reading,

Sophy Thompson, Laurence Stasi, Éléonore Thérond, and Sébastien Ratto-Viviani for the enormous amount of help they gave me, and Alexia for her cosseting and all the delicious food with which her "Bon Mam's" plied me.